D1073215

Information Technology in Social Work
Practice Skills for the 21st Century

Phyllis Schiller
Northern Arizona University

TOURO COLLEGE LIBRARY
Midtown
WITHDRAWN

PEARSON

Boston   New York   San Francisco
Mexico City   Montreal   Toronto   London   Madrid   Munich   Paris
Hong Kong   Singapore   Tokyo   Cape Town   Sydney

MT

Copyright © 2005 Pearson Education, Inc.

All rights reserved. No part of the material protected by this copyright notice may be reproduced or utilized in any form or by any means, electronic or mechanical, including photocopying, recording, or by any information storage and retrieval system, without written permission from the copyright owner.

To obtain permission(s) to use material from this work, please submit a written request to Allyn and Bacon, Permissions Department, 75 Arlington Street, Boston, MA 02116 or fax your request to 617-848-7320.

ISBN   0-205-42432-5

Printed in the United States of America

10 9 8 7 6 5 4 3 2 1   09 08 07 06 05 04

3/8/07

This book is for:

- ➤ **My parents who sacrificed;**
- ➤ **My partner who supported;**
- ➤ **My brother who dreamed; and**
- ➤ **My students who critiqued**

I thank each and every one of you.

CONTENTS

Preface

Why Learn Information Technology In Your Social Work Role?

To think of computers and social work in the same breath is to think of apples and olives. What does working with a machine have to do with helping people? Yet, as we venture into the 21st century, the blending of these two disparate skills is essential for effective client services and agency functioning. Technology's increasing presence in social work agencies is setting the stage for changes so fundamental that, in one way or another, they will impact everything we do in social work as we move into this new century.

Gingerich and Green (1996) in an edited book on future issues in social work state that "by the year 2000 those who chose social work because it was not viewed as a technical field of practice will be faced with making critical career decisions, either to embrace information technology or to choose another profession" (p.26). [1] Likewise, most small, non-profit human service agencies (especially in rural areas) do not use sophisticated, automated information systems for agency management or to facilitate client service delivery. In fact, in many cases, the use of computers is relegated to word processing tasks and rudimentary budget generation.

The year 2000 has come and gone and we still, as a profession, lag behind in the education and training of a skilled IT (information technology[2]) social work workforce. Various sectors in social work education have championed the need for this skill to be included in core curriculum. Dick Schoech of the University of Texas at Arlington is a

---

[1] Gingerich, W. & Green, R. (1996). Information Technology: How Social Work is Going Digital. In P. Raffoul, Future Issues for Social Work Practice (pp.19-28). Boston: Allyn & Bacon.

[2] Information technology is defined as the use of computer and web applications and tools.

pioneer and early adopter of IT for social work. He is the founder and editor of The

Journal of Technology in Human Services and the webmaster of Computer Use in Social

Service Network: http://www2.uta.edu/cussn. There is also the very proactive

Technology and Distance Education Committee of the Association of Baccalaureate

Program Directors (BPD).[3] Social work educators on this committee continually present

papers and demonstrations of various IT skills at annual conventions. Yet, many social

work programs do not have content on IT skills integrated into their curriculum. If they

do, it is mainly on effective utilization of Internet skills and not on the application of

software programs to enhance their practice with clients and agency operations.

As a result of this lack of IT training in social work curriculum, some social work

students and agency workers are computer phobic and many are "computer ignorant"

with regard to how to effectively utilize information technology in an agency. There is a

litany of professional journal articles and books dating from the mid-80's to the present

that describe the need for social workers to be computer literate for agency purposes:

(Butterfield (1983); Bogal-Allbritten & Allbritten (1985); Miller (1986); Glastonbury

(1988); Finn (1988); Cnaan (1989); Pardek & Schulte (1990); Nurius (1991); Schervish

(1993); Resnick (1994); Finn & Lavitt (1995); Gingrich & Green (1996); Karger &

Levine (1999); Schoech (1999); Patterson (2000); and Resnick & Anderson (2002).

Friedman (1998) argues that the tools of technology can assist social workers to work

smarter. When social work students "learn how to use the technology as students, they

will be better able to adapt the experience into their professional lives" (p. 11).[4] Rondero

---

[3] Visit the BPD website for more information about this committee: http://www.bpdonline.org/dnav/7/page.htm.
[4] Friedman, B., Ward, D. & Biagianti, A. (1998). Enhancing student ability to navigate the rapidly changing information environment. Paper presented at the 42nd Annual Program Meeting of the Council on Social Work Education, Chicago, IL.

(1998) states that the presence of computer technology in social work settings no longer ought to be discussed as an option. "Its presence needs to be viewed as a necessity to support the day to day operations of social service agencies in both the public or private non-profit sectors" (p.47).[5] As reported in the NASW News (1999), the 1999 Delegate Assembly of the National Association of Social Workers approved a new policy statement on technology. It contains a strong statement advising social workers to "embrace the notion that technology is becoming integral to competent and responsible professional practice and encourage its members to actively seek opportunities for ongoing education and training in technology." (p. 8).[6]

This book is aimed at providing you with the tools and skills to become a 21st century social worker!

What You Will Learn and How You Will Learn IT

You will learn various aspects of information technology (IT) to enhance your skill in using the computer and Internet for more helpful client services and for your own effectiveness in completing agency tasks. IT is defined as the use of computer and Internet tools.

The Context: The doors of a new, non-profit social service agency in a rural county in a southwestern state will be opening soon. It is located in a city of 50,000 and

---

[5] Rondero, V. (1998). Computer Technology in Social Work Settings: Issues, Considerations and Implications for the Profession. In Information Technology for Social Work Practitioner's and Educator's Conference Proceedings (pp.4 0-50). Columbia, SC: School of Social Work, University of South Carolina.

[6] NASW News. (1999). Five Added, 17 Revised, October, 1999, p.8.

serves a catchment area of over 100 miles, including several surrounding smaller communities. It is called Alpine Community Mental Health Center (Alpine CMHC).

The Practice Skills to be Learned:

➤ **Chapter 1: Information Technology and Agency Application.** You will have a refresher course on how to operate and maintain your computer. As a small, non-profit agency, there are no "tech" people hired. You will also learn about your operating system (Windows XP) and main features of your application software (MS Office XP).

➤ **Chapter 2: Word and Agency Application** and **Chapter 3: Graphics and Agency Application.** With the agency opening in a few weeks, you need to create an agency letterhead, agency description and brochure, agency forms (such as progress notes ecomaps, flow charts, and memo templates), and a newsletter.

➤ **Chapter 4: The Internet and Agency Application.** After a review of basic Internet and Web operations, you will learn how to use search tools to find information and resources for your clients and to provide you with background information for agency reports and grants. Not all the information you find will be of value to you; you need to critically evaluate websites for valid and accurate information. You will learn how to access resources for evidence based practice. You will learn how to protect clients' confidentiality and security when you use your computers to surf the Web and use email. You will learn about the ethical issues of an emerging technology called videoconferencing that is currently being used for assessment and intervention.

➤ **Chapter 5: Spreadsheets and Agency Application.** Once Alpine CMHC is opened, you will be creating and using a budget, developing "what if" projections for program planning and staff needs, and utilizing computerized single case designs for client evaluation.

➤ **Chapter 6: Databases and Agency Application.** You will create and manage a client database and a computerized information and referral directory of area agencies. You will learn how to integrate these databases with form letters using the mail merge function so your mass mailings will be individualized.

➤ **Chapter 7: Slide Shows and Agency Application.** At the end of the "year", you will produce an annual report as a PowerPoint presentation to the agency's board of directors which will include many of the data you generated in earlier chapters as well as new data on client profiles.

To master these skills, you will learn how to effectively utilize the major tools of MS Office XP; including Word, Excel, Access, PowerPoint, and the omnipresent toolbars—Draw and Picture to create these documents.[7] The Microsoft Office suite was chosen to demonstrate the skills and tools you need because it is the most widely used software package in the agencies where you will be working.[8] You will not be shown every feature of every program—this approach would teach you by rote without understanding why you are doing it. You will be shown only those features that you will need in utilizing your IT skills for effective agency and client work.

---

[7] Microsoft is releasing an upgrade to MS Office 2003 during the writing of this book. In reading the previews of this upgrade, I have made the decision to stay with Office XP in the illustrating of practice skills for two reasons: 1) most of the changes benefit large organizations that want to tie into corporate databases so Outlook (which we are not using) has been much improved; 2) there are only minor changes to the Office applications that we are using. If you are currently using Office 97 or Office 2000, I would suggest you consider upgrading to Office XP (Office 2002) now because these older versions will get less support. Screen shot(s) reprinted by permission from Microsoft Corporation.

Most social workers, like you, have never been taught in their professional education or taught themselves these skills as needed. When you graduate and start working in the field, you might have apprehension and reluctance to use computers to try new skills to enhance your work with clients and to improve your ability to more efficiently perform agency tasks. A big mistake! This book is a training/retraining for you!

How to Use This Book

The format of the book puts in plain words and screen shots a step-by-step process for using the software in agency applications. This process is easy to follow. Each major task is explained in detail and is often followed by a practice lesson that will help you apply the learning immediately.

Please note the following instructions to successfully work through the IT skills in this book:

1. You will download files from the companion website (see #8). Put these files in a newly created folder called **ITSW** on your local disk (C:). You will be recreating many of these files and using some files as is. When you create your own documents, compare what you have done to the originals to see how well you did.

2. *Italicized* words in manual are to be typed.

3. **Bolded** words are for emphasis.

4. Expressions with **Word(s)>>Word(s)** indicate an action item; for example, File>>Print means go to File menu and select Print.

5. I have created a **Notes** column to the left of the content for you to jot down tips, hints, and reminders of how to best utilize a skill or tool.

6. Throughout the book there will be **tips** that will inform your use of IT.

7. *Research Navigator Guide for the Helping Professions* by Kjorness & Barr (2004) and also published by Allyn and Bacon is bundled free with this book. It contains a listing of social work websites that covers the breadth and depth of resources that will be useful in your practice. It also has an excellent discussion of search engines and how to evaluate websites. I will be referring to this text in sections of Chapter 4: The Internet and Agency Application.

8. This book has an accompanying website: http://www.ablongman.com/schiller. The site has two sections:

   a. **For Students:** practice files that will be used and modified during the course, sample assignments and their results for each of the book's chapters, and new and updated links to social work areas in Chapter 4.

   b. **For Instructors:** a detailed and complete instructor manual that includes: student practice files; assignments, their results and grading templates; a sample syllabus; suggestions for integrating IT skills across the foundation curriculum; and a Q/A link directly to the author for questions about the content of the book, website, and logistics of the course itself.

About the Author

I am a professor in the Social Work Program at Northern Arizona University (NAU) in Flagstaff, Arizona. I received my Master of Social Work at New York University and my Doctor of Social Work at the University of Utah. I have been at NAU since 1980 and have participated in the beginnings of what is now a fully Council on Social Work Education accredited undergraduate social work program.

What makes a social worker focused on helping people turn into a "computer nerd"? Since the early 90's, I have experienced a self-transformation from an IT illiterate to an IT competent social worker. An old dog CAN learn new tricks!

A sabbatical project in 1992 to learn about the Internet became a journey that has led me to the publishing of this book. A few years after my sabbatical, I offered an experimental course in computer usage in a social agency setting. A local agency that wanted to be "computerized" served as an exemplar. Students got jobs based, in part, on their newly acquired computer skills. The course became required for all social work majors at NAU and is now offered online. This book is the result of many years of testing, revision, and refinement of earlier versions. I see myself in a social work **broker** role: linking people with the resources they need. In this sense, you are my client system. Computers and the Internet are tools for you to use with the people you serve.

Get ready to become a 21st century social worker!

Chapter 1
Information Technology and Agency Application

HARDWARE, SOFTWARE, AND YOU: ARE YOU COMPATIBLE?

This introductory chapter will provide a basic knowledge of your computer hardware, the software that operates your computer (Windows XP) and the software that you use to run applications (MS Office XP). Through tips and shortcuts, you will be able to optimize your computer's performance and customize your software to fit your own unique needs. Please note that this is not an exhaustive overview of techniques to increase your computer competence. There are many books available to address this need: Brown (2001); Wang (2001); and Kinkoph (2003).

Instead, the specific tips and techniques that have been chosen are meant to improve your efficiency within the agency setting. A caveat— there is always more than one way to perform any task in Windows and Office. If you like trying out alternative techniques, go ahead. The more you know about your computer and its software, the more you will feel empowered and less fearful to use them.

The end result will, hopefully, leave you more technologically competent where the computer and its software become compatible tools with you in your professional practice.

In this chapter, you will learn:

- Hardware description
    - Know your computer and its components
    - Your hard drive and defragmentation

- Windows tips
    - Installing/removing software programs
    - Adding and removing program shortcuts
    - Arranging files for maximum visible information
    - Taskbar shortcut: quick access to frequently used files

- Microsoft Office tips
    - Menus
    - Customizing Options to meet your needs
    - Customizing Toolbars
    - Online Help: Office Assistant and more
    - Navigational functions

- Using special characters to enhance your documents
- Using the thesaurus

HARDWARE DEMYSTIFICATION: KNOW YOUR COMPUTER

- What version of Windows operates your machine?
- How much memory do you have and why do you need a lot of it?
- What components do you have in your computer?
- How big is your hard drive?

Let's explore your computer:

With your mouse, right click on **My Computer >>Properties**

A window with many tabs opens. The default tab is **General.** What you do you see?

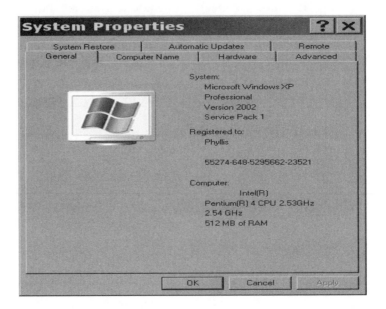

- **MS Windows XP**: Windows is your operating system. It is the software that runs your computer. Without an operating system, your computer would not work. Think of it as the engine in your car. Previous versions of Windows include Windows 2000, NT, and 98. For stability and to minimize crashes, use the latest Windows version.

- **Pentium 4 CPU 2.53GHz:** Pentium is the brand name chip for the central processing unit (CPU) with a processing speed of 2.53 GHz. The higher the number, the faster the computer will perform its operations.

- **512 MB of RAM:** Memory that is installed on this computer. Memory is probably the most important part of the hardware. It enables you to do multi-tasking—performing more than one operation at the same time, such as having more than one application open and then copying and pasting images between the documents of the two applications. If you do not have enough memory to perform these tasks, than a dialog box will appear on your computer and tell you that the operation cannot be completed due to insufficient memory.

  How much memory do you need? As much as you can afford. Memory is cheap. It comes in modules: 16MB, 32MB, 64MB, 128MB, 246MB, 516MB. Do you see a pattern? Yes, these modules double in size.

Go to **Hardware Tab:** Computer Components—The Device Manager button:

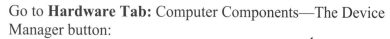

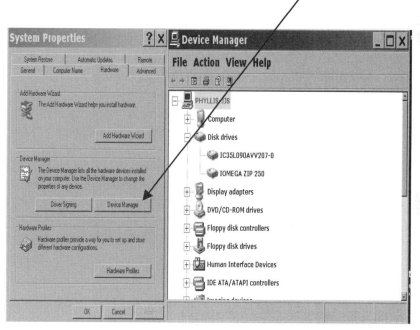

- The **device manager** informs you of the various components you have installed on your computer. Clicking on the + sign will show you the actual brands of your various devices. Being able to identify these components (floppy drive, zip drive, monitor, etc.) will help speed up repair and replacement procedures.

Automatic Updates Tab: Ensures that you receive the latest updates for Windows and downloads them automatically.

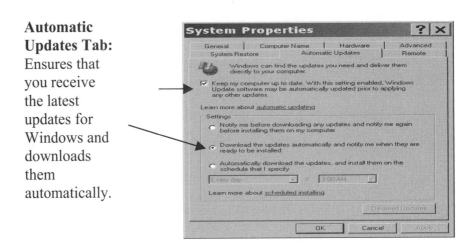

Your Hard Drive: This is a space inside your central processing unit (CPU) not unlike a file cabinet where your files and programs are stored. You need to check its capacity occasionally because it can become full just like a file cabinet. It can also become disorganized. When this happens, it takes longer for you to open and close files. It needs maintenance or defragmentation.

- **Description of Hard Drive: Open my computer>>select C drive>>right click on properties**

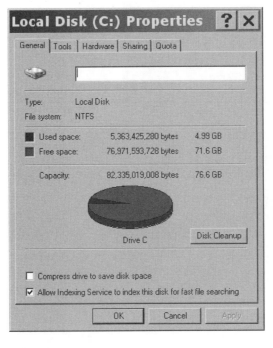

The **general tab** describes your hard drive. It also visually displays the size of your hard drive and how much space you have used and how much space you have left. This is useful so you can decide when it is time to delete unnecessary files, move files to other backup devices, or when to upgrade to a larger hard drive.

- **Defragmentation of Hard Drive:** Fragmentation refers to the condition of a hard disk in which files are divided into pieces scattered around the disk. Fragmentation occurs naturally when you use a disk frequently, creating, deleting, and modifying files. Over time, this process slows down your computer and the operations you normally perform. You need to defragment your hard drive on a regular basis—usually once a month. How?

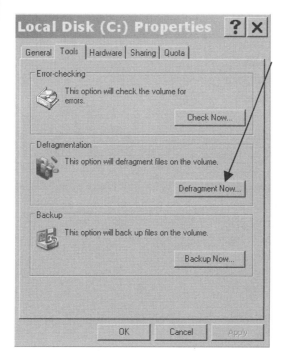

Click on Tools **tab** and then the **Defragment now…** button. Go to action>>analyze and then defragment. Sit back and watch. If you have never done this before, it might take awhile—a few hours. Once you have done it, repeat on a monthly basis. It will not take so long after the initial time. You will have a smooth running machine. Don't be afraid to do this. Your machine will love you!

WINDOWS TIPS: GETTING STARTED AND SAVING TIME

Windows XP is the software that operates your computer and other hardware such as printers, fax machines and external drives. It also is the link between your hardware and your application software, MS Office.

In this section, you will learn how to install and remove software, make shortcuts to programs from the start menu and quick launch toolbar, organize files, and create taskbar shortcuts.

Installing a program to your computer. Almost all new programs today come on a CD-ROM. When you insert it into your drive, Windows should automatically run the setup program for you.

However, if the setup does not start or the program comes on a floppy disk, the following steps will show you how to install the program.

a. Open the Control Panel. Click **start>>control panel** and double-click the **add/remove programs** icon.

b. Add New Programs. Click the **add new programs** button and click the **CD or floppy** button to install the program from the disk. Click next to skip the initial welcome page of the wizard that appears.

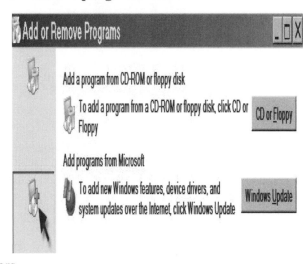

c. Finish. Windows searches both your floppy and CD-ROM drives for a setup program. If it finds one, the path to the program is displayed for your OK. Click **Finish** button to launch the setup program.

d. Restarting. Different programs have different installation routines. Some require that you restart your computer. It is always best to **close** any work you have open and **exit** any running programs before installation procedures.

Removing or uninstalling a program.

a. Open the Control Panel. Click **start>>control panel** and double-click the **add/remove programs** icon.

b. Select a program for removal and click **change/remove.**

c. Follow the onscreen instructions until done.

Shortcuts to programs. Certainly you can put a shortcut to programs on your desktop and just click on it to start your application. What happens over time, however, is that the desktop gets so crowded you spend your time just looking for it to click on it. There are less cluttered ways to easily access your frequently used programs and keep your desktop clean at the same time.

a. **Add a program to Start menu:**

You can quickly access any program you use frequently by adding it to the Start menu. By clicking on the Start Button at lower left of your screen (keyboard equivalent is **Windows** keys located on both sides of the space bar), you can see it immediately and open the program without the circuitous route of clicking on My Computer, clicking the C drive, clicking the Program folder, and so on or going to Start>>Programs>>your program choice.

Here's how to add **Word** to your start menu:

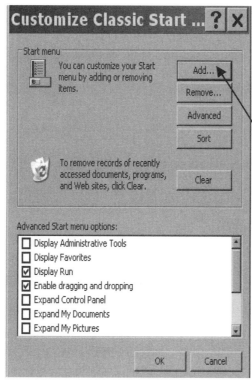

1) Start Button (lower left of screen)>>settings >>task bar and start menu>>select start menu tab
2) Click customize button and select **add**
3) Create shortcut window opens. Click browse to find **Word** in your MS Office folder within your program folder on your C drive in your my computer:

"C:\Program Files\MicrosoftOffice\Office10\WINWORD.EXE", click OK and then next.

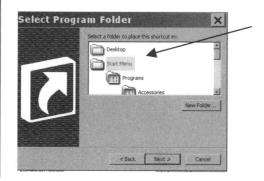

4) Select **start menu** in dialogue box, click next, type the name for your shortcut, *Word,* and then click finish.
5) Go to Start Menu and you will see the **Word** shortcut.

b. To remove a program shortcut from Start Menu:

1) Select the program you want to delete

2) Right click on your mouse and choose **delete**

3) A dialogue box appears and click the delete shortcut button (you will not be deleting the program, only the shortcut)

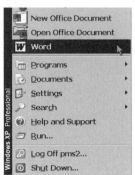

c. Shortcuts to Programs: Quick Launch (QL) Toolbar

It is situated between the Start button and the taskbar

and is actually an extension of the Start menu. You can start programs/utilities located in it just by clicking on its icon. And you can add applications to it.

If you do not see the QL toolbar on your screen, then you need to open it.

1) Start Button>>settings>>task bar and start menu>>select task bar tab and click on Show Quick Launch **or**

2) Right click on any empty space on taskbar, choose toolbars and select Quick Launch.

Do not add too many icons to the QL toolbar as it will take space from your taskbar. Choose only those applications that you use **most** frequently.

Practice: Add MS Word to the Quick Launch toolbar.

1) Click the Show Desktop button on the Quick Launch toolbar to minimize all open windows and to access the desktop if you are not already at desktop.

2) Open the Start menu and locate the MS Word shortcut

3) Using the right mouse button, drag the shortcut onto the right edge of the Quick Launch toolbar.

4) When you release the mouse button, a shortcut menu appears. Select *Copy Here* command.

5) The Word icon should appear on the toolbar.

6) You can change the order of the icons in the Quick Launch toolbar by simply dragging the desired icon to the location you want.

7) You can rename your QL toolbar icons by right clicking on the desired icon and selecting rename.

8) You can remove the icon from the toolbar by simply right clicking and selecting delete.

File Organization. Files and folders can be viewed in several ways: as thumbnails, tiles, icons, a list, or details.

When you start adding files to a folder, it is most helpful to get as much info as possible about them and to find them easily. This information includes file size, type of file, and date last modified.
To get this view, choose **Details** and arrange icons by **Type.**

Practice: Transfer your practice files from the book's companion website to a newly created folder on your hard disk.

1) Make a new folder on your C drive; for this book, it will be named ITSW

2) Download the files from http://www.ablongman.com/schiller to your newly created folder, ITSW

3) Arranging your files with maximum information visible. Select **View**

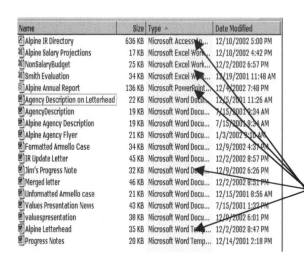

4) Select **details** as it will display the file size, type, and date last worked on

5) Arrange files by **type** to find documents easily

Taskbar Shortcut: Putting frequently used folders/files on taskbar for quick access

When you are working on certain folders/files for a project, it is convenient to get to them quickly. To get to the ITSW folder, what do you have to do?

Open My Computer>>Open C Drive>>Select ITSW folder

Want a quick way?
1) Right click on empty space on taskbar>>toolbars>>new toolbar

2) Choose ITSW folder to open and click OK

3) Note that all files within ITSW are now easily accessible

4) To delete from taskbar, right click on empty space on taskbar>>toolbars>>deselect ITSW

MICROSOFT OFFICE XP REFRESHER AND TIPS

The following techniques apply to all the Office applications that you will use. They are meant to save you time and to customize the programs to your own, unique needs. They include maneuvering menus, utilizing recently used file lists, customizing options and toolbars, navigational functions, using special characters to enhance your documents, and using the thesaurus.

Menus

    a.   File>>Edit>>Insert: You can also open a menu by holding down the <u>Alt</u> key and press the underlined letter of menu you want

    b.   Keyboard shortcuts are shown to the right of the menu options. Learn the ones you use the most to save time. Here a few of the more common shortcuts:
        1) Ctrl P: print
        2) Ctrl S: save
        3) Ctrl C: copy
        4) Ctrl X: cut
        5) Ctrl V: paste
        6) F7: spelling

    c.   An ellipse (…) leads you to a dialog box: Look at PRINT under File Menu
        1) squares: can select all (select options like background printing and reverse order)
        2) round circles: can select only one
        3) drop down menus: arrow and click
        4) options: reverse printing, etc.

    d.   To show full menus: One of the most annoying features that Microsoft introduced is the delayed menu feature. When you go to a menu, it will only show the most recently used commands unless you wait three seconds or click on the double chevron at the bottom of the list.

        Turn off this feature! **Tools>>Customize>>Options**>

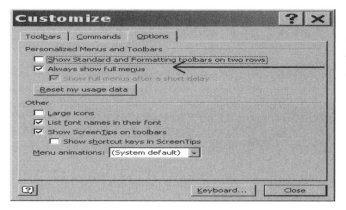

check
Always Show Full Menus

Customizing your computer by using options

There are many choices that you can make to change the way your programs work for you. Review each tab for every application and select what you want. While this might take a little time upfront, the long-term benefits are worth it. Here are just a few suggestions:

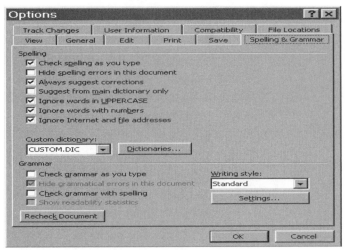

a.   **Tools>> Options >> Sp&Gr.** Make sure you check **Check spelling as you type**.

b.   **Tools>> Options>>General.** Change recently used file list to <u>9</u>. Allows you to access files you recently worked on after going somewhere else. What it does is keep track of the last number of files you have opened in this application and puts that list at the bottom of the File menu. Simply click on the File menu and select the file from the list displayed.

c.   **Tools>> Options>>Save>>turn on auto recovery.** You can further protect your work by using the AutoRecover feature to periodically save a temporary copy of the file you're working on. To recover work after a power failure or similar problem, you must have turned on the AutoRecover feature before the problem occurred. You can set the AutoRecover save interval to occur more frequently than every 10 minutes (its default setting). Set it for 3 minutes, especially during monsoon season.

d.   **Tools>> Options>>File Location tab in Word; the General Tab in Excel; the Save Tab in PowerPoint>>My Documents to C/.** Opens the C drive instead of My Documents as the first choice to save files when you click save. Don't clutter you're My Documents folder with files you ought to organize in folders on your C drive.

e. **Tools>> Options>>Edit>>Drag-and-Drop text editing**.
    Allows you to cut or copy data from one open file to
    another open file by merely selecting the data and
    dragging it to the other file.

Practice: Drag and Drop.

1) Open Word file: *Alpine Agency Description* and Excel file:
   Salary Projections from your taskbar toolbar folder **ITSW**
   (see page 10).

2) Right click on a blank area of the task bar.

3) Alternately select cascading, horizontal, and vertical views to
   see what happens.

4) Choose the vertical view.

5) Select name and title columns from Salary Projections
   worksheet.

6) Hold down the ctrl key on lower left of keyboard and drag
   this selected data below data in the word document. (The ctrl
   key copies and pastes; just dragging the data cuts it from the
   original file).

7) Close both documents without saving them.

You can customize your toolbars. At the top of the screen, there are
toolbars that contain buttons that are actually shortcuts to various menu
commands. Since there is not enough room for all the possible menu
commands, only the most popular buttons are there. But you have the
ability to control what buttons appear there.

a. Want to put the insert date on your standard toolbar since you
    type many letters to clients or other agencies?

Here's how:

**Practice: Move date button to standard toolbar and change default
date (9/7/03) to September 7, 2003.**

1) Tools>>customize>>toolbar tab>>select standard toolbar

2) Click on Commands tab. You will see two lists. The list on the left is a list of the toolbar button categories, basically corresponding to the menu items across the top of the screen. The list on the right is a list of the toolbar button commands than can be placed on the toolbar.

3) Select **Insert>>Date**

4) Drag the Date button to toolbar before page preview icon

5) Click on the button: 6/8/2004

6) Click on **Insert>>Date/Time on Menu bar** and change to text date. Click default.

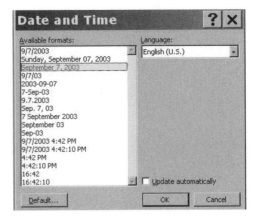

7) Click on date button again: September 7, 2003

b. Change *saves* to *save as* on the toolbar.

Why? *Save as* works the same as *save* the first time you use it. You name the file and put it in the desired folder. After this initial save, using *save as* gives you the option of replacing the existing file, saving the file with a different name, in a new folder or in another format. It offers many more options to saving a document than the simple save command. Here's how:

Practice: Change *save* to *save as* on standard toolbar.

1) <u>Alt</u> V or View>>Toolbar>>customize

2) Select standard>>commands

3) File>>Save As…

4) Drag to standard toolbar next to save and drag off
   save

What icons do you want on your toolbars?

Help>> Show Office Assistant and other tips

You can save money and time by using the Onscreen Office
Assistant. No more buying books on how to use Office. It's free and
right at your fingertips! USE IT!

   a. **Help>> Show the Office Assistant**
   b. Right click on clip, view Options tab
      and select what you want as aids

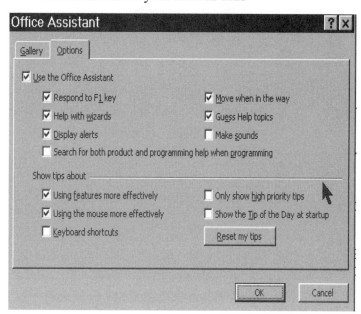

   c. Ask a Question is the primary way to access help in
      Office. **Help>>Microsoft Word Help or F1 key.** A box
      opens. Type a few words in plain English and the
      program returns a list of up to nine topics related to your
      question.

Practice: **Find out how to use Format Painter.**

1) Click F1 key and type
   Format Painter in box

2) Select Search

3) Select *Apply strikethrough formatting*

4) Opens Onscreen Help Manual

5) If you don't find the answer you're looking for, the Ask a Question box is backed up by a

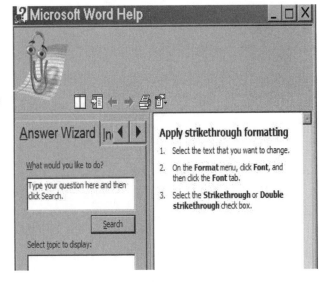

searchable table of contents, by an index in the form of a keyword search, and by the Answer Wizard, which extends the capabilities of the Ask a Question box.

Spelling Tip: rest cursor on problem word and <u>right click</u>   Example: type cultivate. Put cursor over this red-lined word>>>spelling options appear.

Use **UNDO** whenever you make a mistake. You can reverse as many actions as you want. Don't worry!

Task Pane: A new feature in Office XP

The task pane is a window that resides to the right of your open files in any of the Office programs that provides quick access to common functions of that particular program.

> **Task Pane (View menu)**
>
> Displays the task pane, an area where you can create new files, search for information, view the contents of the clipboard, and perform other tasks.

To open the task pane, go to **View>>Task Pane.**

For example, in Excel the task pane looks like this:

You can switch between task panes by clicking the down arrow and click the task pane you want or you can close the task pane window by clicking on the **X.**

Navigational functions: Use the keyboard to save time

You don't have to use the mouse to do things like open menus, select text, or move the cursor. You may do you work more efficiently if you're not always moving your hand from the keyboard to the mouse.

Select entire document ....Ctrl + A
Go to beginning of current line ....Home
Go to end of current line...................End
Go to beginning of document..............Ctrl + Home
Go to end of document....................Ctrl + End
Go to next word...........................Ctrl + ⟶
Go to previous word....................... Ctrl + ⟵
Go to next page............................Ctrl + PgDown
Go to previous page........................ Ctrl + PgUp

By pressing the **Shift** key while executing one of the navigational commands, the text between the initial point of the cursor to the destination will be selected.

Using special characters to enhance your documents

There are a multitude of symbols and characters that can enhance your documents such as superscripts and subscripts, block elements, number forms, and — (em dashes).

   a.   Go to **Insert>>Symbol or Special Character tab**

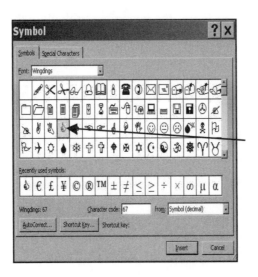

b. On the Symbols tab, pull down the list of fonts and choose **Wingdings.**

c. Select symbol you want, click Insert.

d. You can change the size of the symbol by selecting it and using the font size button:

Using the thesaurus

How often do you find yourself using the same word over and over again in your writing? The onscreen synonym resource, the thesaurus, is always available to you.

a. Click on a word to find a synonym

b. Go to **Tools>>Language>>Thesaurus**

c. Find the word you want and click Replace

Practice: Find a synonym for *service.*

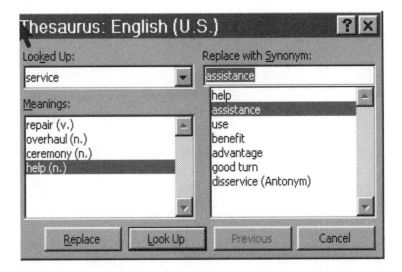

Right Clicking. Almost all the time we only use the left mouse button on the mouse. You select text, menu items, and commands. The **right mouse button** is very powerful and will save you a lot of time. By clicking on it, you can open up shortcuts to many commands and options depending on what you had selected before you clicked on the right button.

For example, if you [select a block of text] and click on the right mouse button, you can quickly access cut, paste, bulleting and numbering, etc. for that selected text.

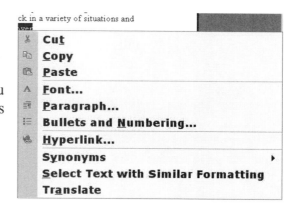

Try the right click in a variety of situations and see what shortcuts you can discover.

Feeling more compatible with your computer and its software now?

Your Notes

Chapter 2
Word and Agency Application

The Word module is the software application you will use most frequently in your work with clients and with agency tasks. Enhancing the look of your documents demonstrates a professional presentation to clients, other agencies, and funding sources. While it is assumed you know basic word processing skills such as cut/paste and moving text, skills such as using headers/footers, bulleting, and indents/tabs will provide a professional appearance to your work.

In anticipation of the opening of the Alpine Community Mental Health Center (Alpine CMHC), you will produce a professional agency description, a flyer stating this description, an agency brochure and newsletter, and a progress notes template for client folders.

To create these documents, you will learn:

- Edit and format
    - Text and paragraphs
    - Format painter
    - Titles and drop caps
    - Bullets and numbering
    - Line spacing
    - Center text on page
    - Borders
- Indents and tabs for creating a table of contents
- Columns, Headers/Footers, Footnotes, and Insert Pictures
- Tables
- Word tips and shortcuts
    - AutoCorrect
    - AutoText
    - Enable AutoComplete
    - Use the Spell Checker
    - Use Word Count

The following two examples illustrate some of the above skills:

An Assessment

Assessment of Angela

Problem Identification

Client is a Hispanic, 21 yo single female self-referred to Guidance Center because of ambivalent feelings surrounding her two month old pregnancy.

Data Collection

Family: Client is one of several children of parents who live in a small, rural community at the other end of the state. Client states they have helped her financially for her schooling, but because of the other children in college, they have helped her all they could. Client has not mentioned pregnancy to them because she did not know what they would say. Reports that she has an aunt and uncle in Flagstone whom she occasionally has weekend dinners.

Significant Other: Hank is a 26 yo divorced father of 4yo son. Client reports they met in class and had been dating about once or twice a week for the past six months. She states they do not socialize with others much and she knows he has been dating other women. At one particular time, she reports he asked her to baby-sit his son while he went out on a date. Her relationship with this child is one of jealousy on the child's part as child makes nasty, cutting remarks to her. Client states that attention toward her by father is the reason for this behavior. She reports that she is fairly certain Hank does not want to marry her. He had never made any commitment to her and she knew he didn't love her. On her side, she didn't think she'd want to be stick with him for the rest of her life. He was a creep in some ways.

School: Client is presently a junior in the social work program at the local university. A college education is important to her. She felt dropping out of school would ruin her life.

Work: Client had worked odd, inconvenient hours at Arby's in the past. Now she was working as a cook several nights a week at Collins Pub.

Present Living Situation: She shares a two bedroom apt. with three other female students. She reports she would have no place to go with a baby and no money. The idea of going on welfare instead of working in welfare was terrifying. Between working, studying, going to classes and seeing Hank, she has little time for much else.

Religion: Client was raised in the Catholic faith, but is not presently practicing it.

Mental Status: Client reports she is totally confused and despondent.

Assessment

Picture of a young female adult who is experiencing cognitive dysfunction. Conflicting values based on religious upbringing vs. recognition of situation present client with inability or unwillingness to make a decision about what to do about the pregnancy. She appears clear about the lack of future with Hank, but this seems to be the only area in which she is. Few linkages with informal support systems contribute to her feelings of depression. Lacks adequate resources such as finances, also. Exploration around options available to her is necessary.

Plan

1. Referral to Planned Parenthood to learn about the options available to her re: pregnancy.
2. Placement in young adult group dealing with life choices at the Center.
3. Reassess her needs and emotional state after she makes a decision about pregnancy.

EDITING AND FORMATTING: TEXT AND PARAGRAPHS

We will begin by replicating the previous assessment from an unformatted version of the assessment.

1. Open the **Unformatted Angela Assessment** file in your ITSW folder.
2. **Text Formatting**: Format>>Font. Review all the changes you can make to text in this dialogue box. Click cancel.

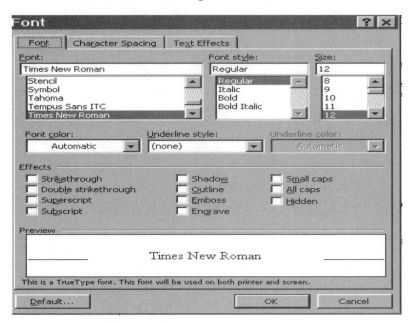

    a. select all (Ctrl A or Edit>>select all). Format>>Font and change font to Times New Roman, 12 pt.
    b. select title and center align, bold and make 14 pt.
    c. click on character spacing tab: expand title character spacing to 1.5 pt

3. **Paragraph Formatting**: On standard toolbar there is a paintbrush

This **Format Painter** tool is a great shortcut for changing the look of paragraphs. You can quickly reformat the assessment using this tool.

    a. Select *Presenting Problem>>*bold and underline
    b. Click on Format Painter and drag icon across the selected text (to copy format)
    c. Click then drag icon across *Data Collection.* Repeat this procedure for *Assessment and Plan.*
    d. Bold *Family* in data collection section. Use the format painter to reformat the other systems as well.
    e. NOTE: If you click elsewhere during the process, then you deselect format painter.

4. Double space between parts of the problem-solving process.

5. Replace the word *client* with the name *Angela:* **Edit>>Replace**

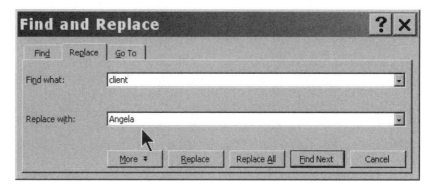

6. Close but **do not save** changes to unformatted Angela assessment as you have a **Formatted Angela Assessment** file already in your folder.

EDITING AND FORMATTING: ADVANCED TECHNIQUES

We will enhance the description of our fictitious agency: Alpine Community Mental Health Center

1. Open the **Agency Description** file in ITSW folder.
2. Open a new document.
3. Tile the two windows vertically (see Drag & Drop, p. 13, #2-4)
4. Copy existing text to new document. Use drag/drop method>>
   a. Ctl A>>selects all text
   b. Ctl + mouse to drag and drop selected text to blank document (drag & drop without ctrl key cuts text from original doc)
5. Close **Agency Description**.
6. Maximize new doc: click on middle button in upper right corner.
7. Title Formatting
   a. Select title
   b. Use Format>>Font >>Bold, 20 pt., Green, Shadow
   c. Use Format>>Font >>Character Spacing>>Spacing>> Expanded >>1.5 pt.
8. After title, hit enter three times.
9. First Paragraph Formatting
   a. Select paragraph by putting cursor in paragraph and clicking three times or moving mouse to left of paragraph and double clicking
   b. Bold, 14 pt and justify(see alignment icons next to **B/U** on Formatting Toolbar)
   c. **Format>>Drop cap** first letter of paragraph 3 lines

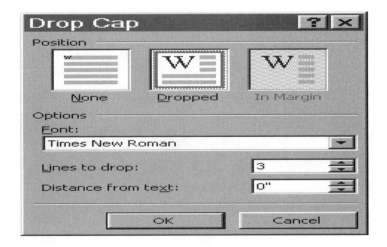

10. After paragraph, hit enter twice.
11. Bold and 14 pt. *Specific Services include:*

12. Select entire list and Bold, 14 pt. and **Bullet List**
    a. Format>>Bullets and Numbering and select

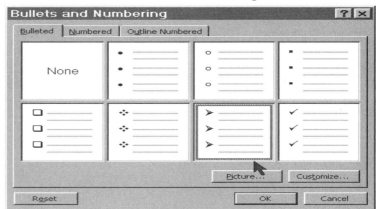

    b. If you want to change the look of the bullet, then click customize

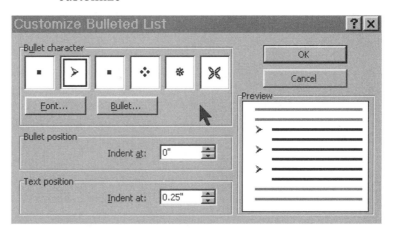

    c. Reformat line spacing to **double spacing** Format>>Paragraph

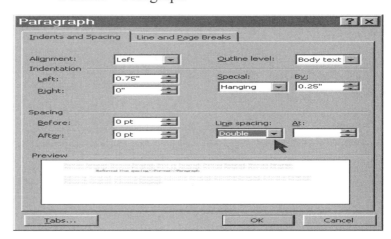

13. **Center all the text on page**
    a. Select all text (ctrl A or edit>>select all, remember?)
    b. File>>Page Setup>>Layout

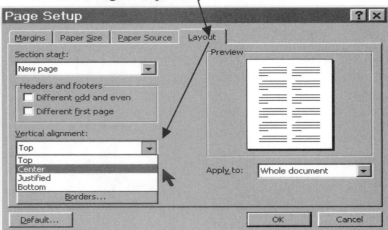

14. OOPS! Dropped T did not move. Select T>>put cursor on its border until it becomes a crosshair and move to correct position before paragraph. (The T became an image when it was converted to Drop Case.)
15. Save as *Alpine Agency Description 1* to your ITSW folder.

16. Make a **flyer of document** by putting a border around it!
    a. Reopen **Alpine Agency Description 1**.
    b. Format>> Borders and Shading…
    c. Click on Page Border tab.
    d. Select **Box**, then **Art**>>scroll to **alpine trees** and click OK.

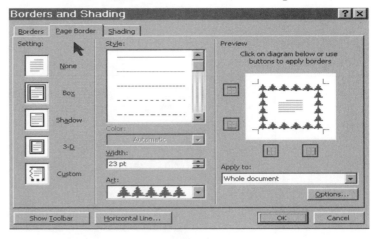

17. Click print preview icon [icon] to see your work.
18. Save as *Alpine Agency Flyer 1.*
19. Close all files.

BULLETS AND NUMBERING

A bullet is a dot, number, or symbol used to highlight points of information or to itemize a list. Using this feature makes reading a document easier and gives flyers and announcements more pizzazz.

You were introduced to bullets and numbering in the previous section on formatting the agency description. Here you will be shown how to utilize its components to your best advantage.

Bullets and numbering lets you:

Numbering and bulleting on format toolbar

1. Create numbered paragraphs.
- Create bulleted paragraphs.
➢ Use symbols instead of the traditional bullet.

1. Reopen **Alpine Agency Flyer**
2. Select the bulleted list
3. Copy into a new document and
4. **Let's play** (I have reformatted the spacing and font size of the list below to conserve space on this page of the book).

➢ information and referral
➢ outpatient counseling for families, groups, and individuals
➢ educational community programs about mental health issues
➢ 24hr. hotline
➢ follow-up services
➢ adoption services

Practice: Change the bulleting to pictures.

1. Select all (ctrl A; got the keyboard equivalent by now?)
2. Go to Format>>Bullets and Numbering...
3. Click Bulleted tab>>Customize>>Select Picture
4. Select the second box in first row and click OK

⚜ information and referral
⚜ outpatient counseling for families, groups, and individuals
⚜ educational community programs about mental health issues
⚜ 24hr. hotline
⚜ follow-up services
⚜ adoption services

Practice: Change the bulleting to symbols.

1. Select all
2. Go to Format>>Bullets and Numbering...
3. Select Bulleted>>Customize... click on character

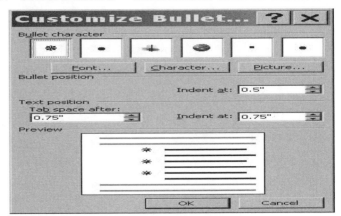

4. Choose a new symbol and click OK

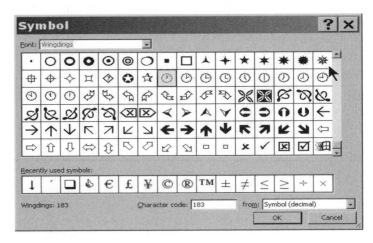

❋ information and referral
❋ outpatient counseling for families, groups, and individuals
❋ educational community programs about mental health issues
❋ 24hr. hotline
❋ follow-up services
❋ adoption services

You can also change the bullet position and text position in the Customize Bullet...dialogue box. See what it looks like in the Preview window.

Close the bullet document. Save it, if you wish, in your ITSW folder.

INDENTS AND TABS

Indents

By default, there are tabs every .5" along the ruler. However, sometimes we need to make our sentences look different, such as inserting quotes into a document. For these effects, we use indents.

First line indent
Hanging indent
Left indent

Open a new document. Type the paragraph below that begins with *Today*... Copy and paste this text below to duplicate its formatting by moving indents as shown in the pictures.

1.

Today we are going to learn how to indent. There are many ways to do this. First, **we will learn left indents**, then we will learn first line indents, then hanging indents, and finally nested indents.

2.

T oday we are going to learn how to indent. There are many ways to do this. First, we will learn left indents, **then we will learn first line indents**, then hanging indents, and finally nested indents.

3.

Today we are going to learn how to indent. There are many ways to do this. First, we will learn first line indents, **then hanging indents**, and finally nested indents.

4.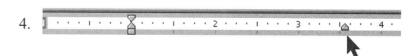

Today we are going to learn how to indent. There are many ways to do this. First, we will learn left indents, then first line indents, then hanging indents, and **finally nested indents.**

Keep this document open.

TABS

This feature allows you to put text exactly where you want it on the page. There are several kinds of tabs that you can place anywhere on the ruler. Look to the far left corner of ruler to find them. You click in this box to toggle through them. They are:

1. **L**   Left tab: text will move to the right

2. **⅃**   Right tab: text will move to the left

3. **⊥**   Center tab: text will move to either side of tab location

4. **⊥**   Decimal tab: will align numbers exactly 34.00
124.00

5. **|**   Bar tab: will put a vertical line on page exactly where the tab is located ⟶

A most useful function of tabs is to make a **table of contents** quickly.
1. Hit enter to move below your indent work and move indents to default left and right margins respectively (as in a new blank document).
2. Set a left tab at 1" and at 4" and a right tab at 3.5".
3. Format>>Tabs>>Select 3.5>>Leader>>2>>Set>>OK.

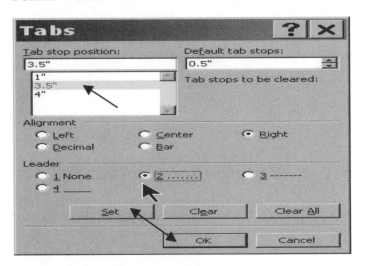

4. Tab and type   *Mission*   tab and type *1....*   *1*
                      Goals............................   *2*
                      Description.....................   *3*
                      Services *4*

Note the exact alignment of the dotted lines and the page numbers. Let the program do it. Don't rely on your eyes. Close without saving.

COLUMNS, HEADERS/FOOTERS, FOOTNOTES, AND INSERT PICTURES

Reports, case assessments, grant proposals, and more will come across as elegant and polished when you apply navigational and presentational aids to your documents. Columns together with pictures/images are especially useful for producing agency brochures and newsletters—whenever you want text to flow without interruption from the bottom of one column and continue on the top of the next.

Here's how to arrange text in newspaper style columns:

1. Open the **Enhancing Social Services** file in ITSW folder.
2. Place cursor at beginning of document. Format>>Columns>> Presets>>2>>check Line between>>Apply to whole doc>>OK.

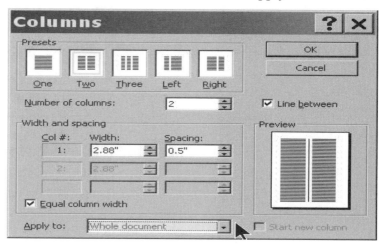

3. View>>Header and Footer. Move cursor over each icon to see what each does.
    a. Header>>insert date, hit enter and type *Enhancing Social Services,* right align both and reduce to 9 pt.

    b. Toggle to Footer>> click on page number icon, center and reduce to 9 pt. DO NOT type in actual page number (1, for example) as all pages will display this number.
    c. Print Preview.

Go to File>>Page Setup>>Layout if H/F text needs adjustment from the edge of paper.

t!p

4. **Add a footnote to document**
   a. Place cursor after **Agencies** in title
   b. Insert>>Reference>> Footnote... and select **Endnote** location
   c. Cut and paste Author info at top of document next to footnote at end of document and change font size to 9 pt.

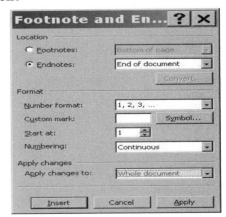

5. **Create a Banner Heading:** Select title, go to Columns and click the single-column layout.

6. **Adding an Image**
   a. Insert>>Picture>>ClipArt
   b. A Task Pane opens. Type light bulb and click search. The results give you many choices. Scroll down to see them.
   c. Put your mouse over one choice and a down button appears. Click on it and a dialogue box opens. Choose **Insert**.
   d. Format **Tight** to left of title using text wrap icon on Picture toolbar>>see page 41, Making the Graphic, #3.
   e. Put cursor over lower right handle of picture and move diagonally inward to reduce size.
   f. Go to print preview. Note the uneven columns on page 2.

7. **Looking Good:** Balance newspaper-style columns on a page.
   a. Click at the end of the columns on p. 2.
   b. Insert>>Break.
   c. Click **Continuous** in Section break types.
   d. Word inserts a continuous section break, which balances the text equally among the two columns.

8. Close file and save as *Enhancing Social Serivices1* in your ITSW folder. Compare your result with the **Column Enhancing SS** file.

 Remember to use the tile windows vertically method from the Task Bar for a quick and easy comparison.

TABLES

You have learned how to align text with tabs. For **brief** paragraphs or documents this is fine. However, you are better off using Word's tables, which organize and present information in a structured, easy-to-read format.

With a table, you can arrange essential text that people can find and read easily. You can either **hide** the table gridlines or choose several kinds of **table formats** for your text. A table consists of rows which displays data horizontally; columns which display data vertically, and cells which are single boxes formed by the intersections of rows and columns. You can use tables for work assignments, program planning, client charting, forms, schedules, process recordings, and more. Here's how:

We are going to make a **progress note template** for you to use when you enter notes into a client's chart. The progress note form will have three columns and several rows. You can add more rows, if needed, as you go.

1. Open a new Word document and go to Table>>Insert Table.

2. Select 3 columns and 4 rows and click OK.

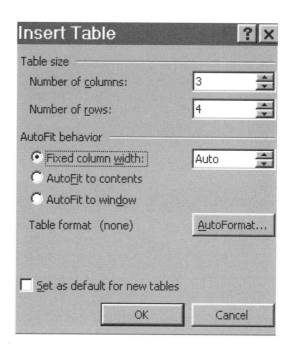

3. Resize the table to fill page, if necessary, by dragging out the lower right corner handle.

4. Type *Date, Observations, Plan* in the first row (tab to go to next column)

Date	Observations	Plan

5. To resize the columns to your text, simply place the cursor over the line until you get the double arrow symbol and drag to size you want.

Notice that the ruler does not have tabs, but instead column dividers. You can also change the column width on the ruler.

Move Table Column

6. Text entry and formatting basics in a table:
   a. Tab to go from one column to next; shift>>tab to go backwards.
   b. To add text in a column, continue typing and the box will automatically expand.
   c. Hitting enter in a box will expand the box.
   d. Text can be formatted as you would in any Word document.
   e. Go to Table>>Insert to add or delete columns or rows.
   f. To merge cells, select the cells you want to merge and go to Table>>Merge Cells.
   g. To split cells, put cursor inside the cell you want to split and go to Table>>Split Cells.

7. Play!

8. To make the table look more professional, go to **Table>>Table AutoFormat...>>**Table Grid 2

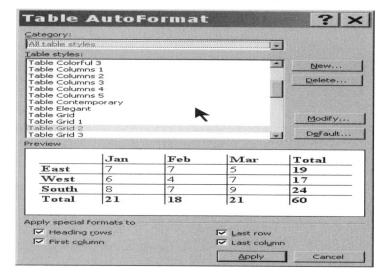

The Result:

Date	Observations	Plan

9. Move table down a ,5" and type *Progress Notes* in 14 pt. bold, and centered.

10. Type *Alpine Community Mental Health Center* as footer, center align, bold and make 9 pt.

11. Preview. Go to Page Setup>>Layout>> Headers/Footers and move Footer to .07".

12. Save as *Progress Notes1* in file name and as **Document Template** in drop down box next to **Save as type.** Click save.

13. Reopen **Progress Notes1** from File>>New Document **or** Start Menu>>New Office Document>>**Progress Notes** and type the following info into table.

Date	Observations	Plan
1/7/04	The client was able to tell his parents that he was not using alcohol anymore with his friends at school. This disclosure enabled the family to begin trusting one another again.	Continue stressing to client to be honest with parents.

14. Save as *Jim's Progress Notes* in ITSW folder.

15. Remember you can use Spell Check and the Thesaurus in Tables also.

Templates have a **yellow** bar at top of document icon. They are preformatted with data you created. They are actually blank documents customized by you. Forget going to the copy store!

WORD SHORTCUTS AND TIPS

AutoCorrect

Can be used to automatically correct misspelled words and incorrect capitalization. You can also use AutoCorrect to quickly insert text, graphics, or symbols by typing in an abbreviation.

1. Tools>>AutoCorrect Options…

2. Select the options you would like to automatically correct. These options allow you to program your common typing errors and have them automatically corrected.

3. **Replace text as you type:** to add a new correction type that is misspelled or an abbreviation (ACMHC can get to be a bear to type all the time) in the **Replace** box. Type in the correct spelling or replacement text in the **With** box.

Practice: Replace *alc* with Alpine Community Mental Health Center.

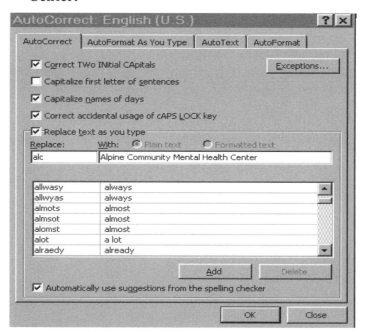

1) Type *alc* in Replace box and *Alpine Community Mental Health Center* in With: box.
2) Click the *Add* button and OK to activate change.
3) Type *alc* followed by a space or enter key and the correction will be made automatically. Thus, alc>> Alpine Community Mental Health Center.
4) To undo AutoCorrect, select the text and use Ctrl Z.

AutoText

   AutoText is another way to insert frequently used text, graphics or symbols. For example, instead of typing your signature and title at end of each letter you write, you can make an AutoText entry for it which will allow you to type only a few key letters. Here's how.

   1. Type your signature as you would at end of letter:
      a. Press enter key twice
      b. Sincerely,
      c. Press enter key four times
      d. Name and title

   2. Select all and Insert>>AutoText>>New

3   Type an acronym (minimum four letters) and click OK.
    Do not use a real word!

4.   Type sigps and hit enter....SAVES TIME?

Practice: Create your own signature!

Enabling AutoComplete

AutoComplete offers on-screen tips as you type to prompt you with possible AutoText entries. Press **enter key** to accept.

1.   Tools>>AutoCorrect Options...

2.   Click on the AutoText tab

3.   Click **Show AutoComplete tips for AutoText and dates** and click OK.

4.   As you type, an AutoComplete tip will appear after you type several letters of an AutoText entry. Hit **enter** to insert the AutoText or keep typing to ignore it.

5.   The computer will complete items such as months of the year and days of the week when you begin typing the word

        August]

        The next board meeting is Augu

Using the Spell Checker

1. **Tools>>Spelling** or **F7 key.** There is no reason to have misspelled words in any of your documents. Always do a spell check before saving a dociment.

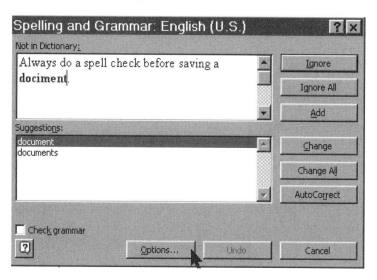

2. You have choices of ignoring the error, adding the word to your custom dictionary where it will not register as a misspelled word, or changing the word with one of the suggestions offered.

3. Go to options and individualize your spelling features.

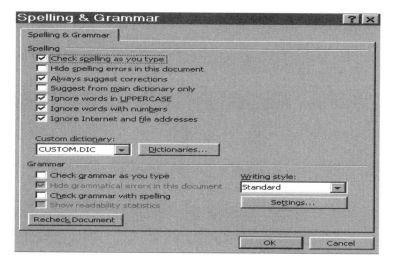

Using Word Count: Tools>>Word Count

When you need to limit your word number such as in an abstract for submission to a journal or funding source, this feature is very handy and saves you time from counting each word. Just select the text you need counted and go to Tools>>Word Count.

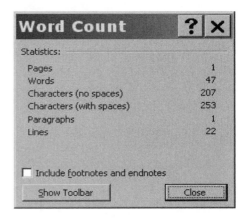

SUMMARY

This chapter demonstrated advanced skills in editing and formatting, bulleting text, using columns for newsletter and brochure creation, placing headers and footers in your documents, inserting images and text wrapping, making templates, creating organized documents with tables, and many Word tips and shortcuts.

Learning these advanced skills in Word will enable you to produce flyers, agency stationary, posters, newsletters, and many other agency document types without the necessity of purchasing a publication program such as MS Publisher. Together with the additional skills in the next chapter on graphics, you will save your agency a lot of money and provide enhanced service to your clients and Alpine Community Mental Health Center.

Chapter 3
Graphics and Agency Application

There are many ways to enhance your agency documents using pictures, images, clip art, WordArt, and the Draw and Picture toolbars. The following techniques will provide you with the tools to make your templates, newsletters, brochures, announcements, or flyers standout.

They can also provide you with the tools to create ecomaps, genograms, and social networking maps for clients' assessment and intervention strategies. In addition, you will learn to use these techniques for organizational chart creation and program evaluation reports in your agencies. Mattaini (1993) produced a text of graphic visualization concepts for assessment, intervention and research. It is an excellent resource on how to apply the tools of this chapter to your practice.

THE AGENCY LETTERHEAD

Want to save money and time buying and inserting your letterhead paper into the printer every time you want to send a formal document? Make your own letterhead (or memo or intake form, etc.) as a Document Template (you already did this for client progress notes form on page 35). You will learn to insert and move graphics, make objects transparent and utilize the Draw and Picture toolbars.

Making the Graphics

1. Open a new Word document

2. **View>>Toolbars>>Select Draw and Picture** and move them to bottom of screen by grabbing the handle at beginning of each toolbar.

3. **Insert>>Picture>>Clip Art**
   a. The task pane opens to the right of your document.
   b. Type *tree* in search box, click search, and scroll until you find this image>>insert

   c. Click on tree and select tight from **text wrap** icon on **Picture toolbar**
   d. Click on tree, click copy and paste the tree twice.

4. Separate the three trees by selecting each one at a time and dragging them apart.
   a. Click on the second tree: **Picture Toolbar>>Color>>Washout**

5. Group the Trees into one image by holding Shift key as you select each one
   a. Be sure to click outside the handle area of each tree to select the others
   b. If dark tree is behind washout go to **Draw>>Order>>Bring Forward**

6. Move into position as shown below and then go to toolbar: **Draw>>Group**; now one set of handles exists.

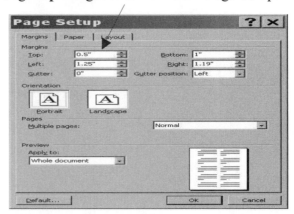

7. Resize by holding shift key at lower right diagonal handle and move inward. (Holding the shift key maintains the image's proportions.)

8. Move image to upper left of document.

Making the Text

Change **top** margin to .5" in File>>Page Setup.

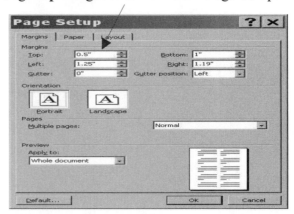

The agency letterhead should be above the 1" default for any document. It will be permanently situated at the top of every page.

1. Do the following **Format>>Font** operations in dialogue box below and then align right, type *alc* and hit enter (remember replace feature in autocorrect on page 37?).

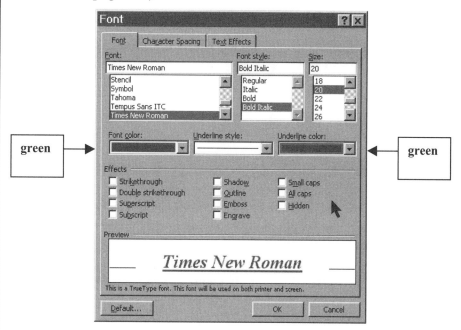

2. Hit enter, **Format>>Font:** 14 pt., green, no underline, and right align and type>> *linking people with the resources they need*

3. Hit enter 2x, 12 pt., green, right align, and type address>>

    123 Leroux St.   Flagstaff, AZ 86001
    (928) 774-1234   (928)774-4321 (fax)
    www.alpinecmhc.org

4. You'll notice that the URL becomes a hot link (blue): *www.alpinecmhc.org.* To remove the hot link, put mouse on the URL, right click and select **Remove Link** in dialog box.

5. Put your cursor over all the icons on the Draw Toolbar to see what they are. Hit enter, select **line** icon from **Draw toolbar** and make a line across bottom of text using **line style>>6 pt**. and **line color>> green.** (Hold shift key when drawing line to keep it straight.)

6. Deselect italic icon, move graphic into place, move cursor below line, left align and make sure text on cursor is set to **font color>>black.** Check margins from page setup to ensure the defaults of 1" on left and 1.25" on right.

7. Save as **Alpine Letterhead** and make sure you save it as **document template.**

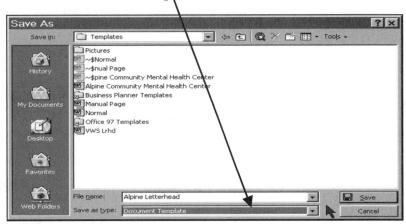

Close after you're satisfied it looks like the letterhead below.

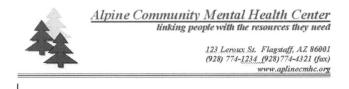

8. The Result: The Agency Letterhead Template.

AGENCY DESCRIPTION ON AGENCY LETTERHEAD

The agency letterhead is actually a blank document with a permanent letterhead at top. This is what a template does. You save the document as you would any other blank Word file. You'll notice it says Document 1-MS Word in upper left of screen when you open it.

1. Click **File>>New...>>Alpine Letterhead** from task pane within a new blank Word document **or Start>>New Office Document>>Alpine Letterhead**

2. Open **Alpine Agency Description** and copy and paste into Letterhead file **or** tile windows vertically and use drop/drag method.

3. In Letterhead file, delete Agency Title from text.

4. Move that T! Print preview and format as needed.

5. Save as *Agency Description on Letterhead1* as a **Word document** in ITSW folder and close all open files.

Other agency templates

Word comes with many special-purpose templates that you can use to save time in your document creation. Some of these include newsletters, letters, memos, faxes, reports, and resumes. To use a template, just choose **File>>New...>>New from template (on task pane)>>General Templates...** and select the template you want from the new dialog box.

Practice: **Create your own personalized memo.**

1. Open new word document. **File>>New>>New from Template>>General Templates>>Memo>>Professional Memo.** Click Template and click OK.

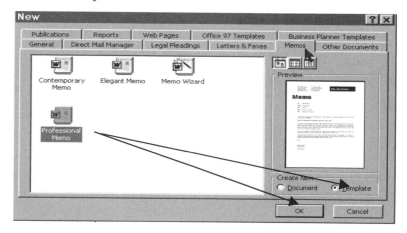

2. Format the document with agency name centered in Company Name box: *Alpine CMHC,* type your own name in From:, delete the CC: line, change font size to 14 pt. in body area, and delete the "How to info" after you have read it. Save as *My Memo* and change *save as* type to **document template.**

3. Next time you want to use it, choose **File>>New>>New from Template>>General Templates>> My Memo or** hit **Start>>New Office Document>>My Memo.**

USING THE DRAW AND PICTURE TOOLBARS

The tools on the Draw and Picture toolbars should be available to you at all times in all Office programs. Make sure they are open and at the bottom of your screen. Go to **View>>Toolbars>>Select Drawing and Picture.**

Review each of the tools on the Draw toolbar.

Holding down the shift key when you draw a rectangle or oval will make a square or a circle, respectively.

Review each of the tools on the Picture toolbar.

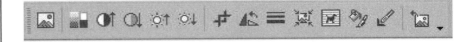

Creating assessment and intervention tools[1]

Ecomaps (Hartman (1978), genograms (Hartman & Laird (1983), or social network maps (Tracy (1993) are visual depictions of clients' person-in-environment contexts and are used for assessment and intervention strategy decisions. The social network map, for example, demonstrates the extent of a client's functional and structural relationships with others. It points to strengths and gaps in the client's social supports. When working directly with your clients, these visual diagrams can be especially useful in developing a sense of mutuality and relationship-building between client and worker.

Using the Draw toolbar, you will learn how to create these tools and share them with your clients.

---

[1] There are two commercial software companies that generate electronic ecomaps and genograms for workers to use in making these assessment tools: WonderWare (http://www.interpersonaluniverse.net/wware.html). It cost is over a $100 and SmartDraw (http://www.smartdraw.com) which helps the worker create ecomaps, genograms, organizational charts and more. It costs over $200. Why pay this if you can do it yourself using the draw and picture toolbars?

Drawing Shapes and Lines

1. Click on oval.

2. Drag the mouse pointer to create the shape. **Hold** the shift key while making oval to make a circle.

Holding the shift key while drawing a shape will make a line straight, a rectangle a square, an oval a circle.

3. Click on circle and choose fill and line colors on the style buttons on the Drawing toolbar.

4. Select green as a fill color and red as a line color.

5. Keep circle selected, go to Fill Color icon, click on carrot to open the dialogue box and choose **Fill Effects.**

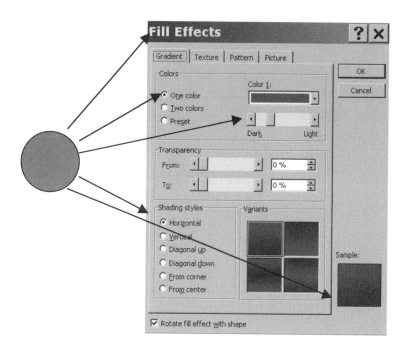

Look at the other tabs on fill effects dialogue box and play with the circle. Your creativity is limitless!

6. To add text inside a shape, click the shape and then click

    text box on the **Draw toolbar** and
    begin typing.
    a. Type *Amy.*
    b. Remove white background: **Fill
        Color>>No Fill** in dialogue box.
    c. Remove black line**: Line Color>>No Line**

7. Lines and their styles are also available on the toolbar:

Practice: **You have the tools to create an ecomap.
Replicate the ecomap below.**

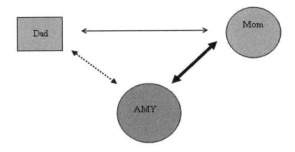

Legend:

.... lines indicate a distant relationship

━━━━━━━━ lines indicate a close relationship

◀━━━━━━━▶ direction of arrows indicate the equality of the
relationship (who gives the most)

▢ a box is male   ◯ a circle is female

8. **Grouping and ungrouping shapes**. By grouping several
    objects, you can treat them as a single object and move the
    combined object as one around on the page.

    a. Hold down
        the shift
        key as you
        click each
        object.

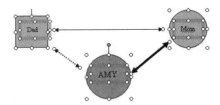

b. Click on the Draw word on the Draw Toolbar, choose *Group*

c. A single set of handles

now surrounds the objects in the group. To ungroup the objects, select the group and then choose *Ungroup* from the Draw drop arrow list on the draw toolbar.

Creating agency organizational charts

A new icon [icon] on the Draw toolbar in Office XP makes creating an organizational chart of your agency very simple. Together with your font manipulation skills, you can customize the chart to fit your unique agency structure.

1. Click on **Insert>>Diagram or Organization Chart** icon on **Draw toolbar**.

2. A dialog box with several selections appears. Choose organizational chart.

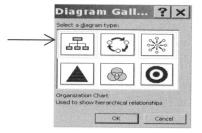

3. The organizational chart appears. When you then click on the chart, an **organizational chart toolbar** appears.

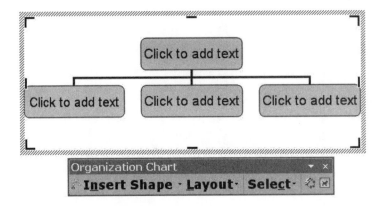

4. The toolbar allows you to manipulate the organizational structure in a number of ways:

    a. **Insert Shape:** select a box and then you can add a coworker, subordinate or assistant connected to that box.

    b. **Layout:** gives you options on the direction and hierarchy of your chart

    c. **Select:** allows you to format more than one cell at one time, be it a level, a branch, the assistants or the connecting lines.

    d. The **Autoformat** icon 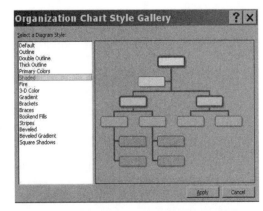 gives you the option of selecting from a multitude of diagram styles.

Practice: Make your own organizational chart. If you are not knowledgeable of an agency's organizational structure, then do one of your family.

WordArt and agency documents

WordArt is specially formatted text that you can display in a number of preset styles. This text, which is really an **image** and, therefore, can be moved around and resized like any image, works well on report covers, title slide of presentations, brochure covers, and newsletter headings.

Several tools are available to help you create and edit WordArt. You can move, resize, and reshape the WordArt using the handles that appear, just as you adjust other images.

We will make the title for the Annual Agency Report using WordArt.

1. Click the WordArt button on the Draw toolbar.

2. Click the style in the 3rd row, 1st column.

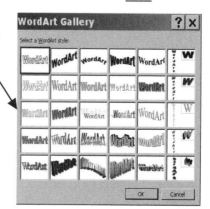

3. Type *Alpine Community Mental Health Center*, change font to Comic Sans MS, and click OK.

Alpine Community Mental Health Center

4. Double click on the graphic and the WordArt toolbar appears.

You can change the size, shape, color, direction, and other aspects of the graphic by clicking on and selecting features in each of the toolbar icons.

5. Play with it!

SUMMARY

Your **draw assignment** will build on your many skills from the Word chapter plus your newly learned skills from the Draw and Picture toolbars in this graphics chapter to create a **tri-fold brochure** for the agency.

You have acquired the IT skills that have helped you prepare agency forms and agency promotional materials. The doors of Alpine Community Mental Health Center are now open. You will begin seeing clients and performing agency tasks.

To enhance your performance in these services, you will learn how to create and use: budgeting, visual client evaluations, projection tools for future planning, client databases, computerized information and referral directories, mail merges, and slide show presentations for community outreach, training, and agency meetings. First, however, a field trip to the Internet is necessary to ensure accurate usage of this resource in your professional practice.

Chapter 4
The Internet and Agency Application

> ➤ A client with epilepsy comes to Alpine Community Mental Health Center dealing with depression. Her license has been taken away because her seizures are not under control. She lives in an area of town without public transportation and has become increasingly isolated. Where can you find support groups for her?

> ➤ You are writing a grant to the state for an intensive home care program for the elderly who live in Coconino County. You need the latest statistics on the county's population broken down by city and age. Where do you find this data quickly?

> ➤ You get a frantic call from a client whose teenage, pregnant daughter just took a few of this client's Zoloft, an antidepressant medication. The client is worried about what effects this might have on the fetus. Where can you rapidly find out about the precautions of this drug?

> ➤ Your client who is struggling with a behavioral pattern of passive-aggressiveness is not responding to your intervention strategy. You want to find the latest research on this topic to look for alternative strategies. Where do you look for it?

> ➤ You want to remind your Coalition on Children agencies of the upcoming meeting on Thursday. How can you do this in one procedure?

The answer to each of these scenarios: The Internet[1]. Online support/discussion groups, databases, websites, and email are various ways the Internet serves as an information source and communication method for you in your agency work.

Learning to use the Internet competently is a skill. It is important for you as social workers to master the Internet in order to:

- serve as brokers, teachers, enablers, advocates, and mediators (BTEAM) for your clients utilizing functional and current information on the Internet in the various knowledge base areas of social work.
- discern valid information from quackery.
- not feel lost and not in control when you look for information.

---

[1] The Internet and the Web are not interchangeable words, but they are similar. Go to the glossary to find out how they differ.

- not use outdated websites and outdated information.
- recognize the ways that security and confidentiality of clients can be violated and learn how to safeguard against this.

There are many excellent books on the Internet and social work: Kardas & Milford (1996); Grant & Grobman (1998); Vernon & Lynch (2000); Martinez & Clark (2001); and Kjosness & Barr (2004).

The packaging of *Research Navigator Guide for the Helping Professions* by Kjosness & Barr with this book will provide you with a very solid and comprehensive base for learning how to use the Internet competently as well as a resource for a multitude of social work related websites.

In this chapter you will learn:

- Browser basics
    - URLs
    - Menus
    - Buttons
    - Error Messages
- How to use the various types of search tools
    - Search engines and Google
    - Subject directories
    - Virtual libraries
- Examples of reference and resource sites in specific social work areas
- How to critically evaluate the websites you find
- How to use the Internet for evidence based practice
- Ethical issues on the Internet and with IT
    - Security and confidentiality
    - The emergence of telehealth

BROWSER BASICS[2]

1. **URLs (Universal Resource Locator)** The unique address of any Web document. May be keyed in Internet Explorer's File>>Open, Address Bar or typed into dialogue box that opens with keyboard shortcut: pressing **Ctrl & O** to retrieve a document.

---

[2] The browser used in this book is Internet Explorer (IE). The explanations about browsers therefore pertain to IE.

There is logic to the layout of a URL:

Type of file (could say ftp:// or telnet://)	Subdomain/Domain name (physical location of site and the type of organization it is)	Path or directory on the computer to this file	Name of file and its file extension (usually ending in .html or .htm)
http://	www.nau.edu/	library/	resources.html

a. Subdomain.**domain** The domain is usually three letters. They tell you **what kind** of site you are visiting:

gov	government; the most reliable and valid
edu	educational institutions; a close follow-up to gov
org	not for profit agencies
com	for profit agencies and companies
mil	military sites
ca	the country Canada
uk	the countries: United Kingdom
~	tilde in address usually indicates a personal page such as a faculty website

b. **Subdomain**.domain The subdomain tells you the actual location you are visiting:

nau.edu   Northern Arizona University
naswaz.org   National Association of Social Workers, Arizona Chapter
aol.com   America Online

c. The backslash (/) after the initial address directs you to other pages on the website: nau.edu/**library**

d. The htm or html extension indicates a specific file: nau.edu/library/**resources.html**

Entering the **correct** URL is vital to successful Internet navigation.

2. **Menus on your browser**

File Edit View Favorites Tools Help

a. **File**>>Print>>Options based on your need; using a portion of a website's info in a paper is easily done by selecting what you want and then choosing *selection* in the print range area in the print dialogue box.

b. **Edit**>>**Find** Locates specific words.

c. **View**>>**Go To** Gives list of sites you have already visited.

d. **Favorites** When you find a site that you visit a lot, click on this button. It saves and organizes sites into your own folders

e. **Tools**>> **Internet Options**

1) Define **Homepage:** insert the website that will open when you start your browser. You must insert the entire URL.

2) Clear **Temporary Internet Files** if you do not want your Web surfing traced.

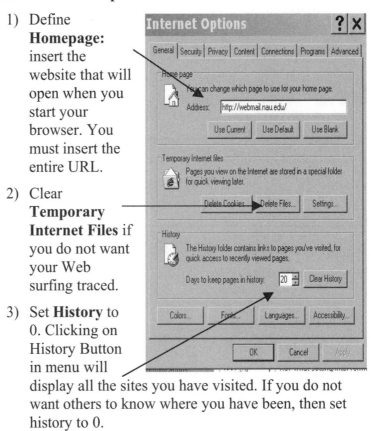

3) Set **History** to 0. Clicking on History Button in menu will display all the sites you have visited. If you do not want others to know where you have been, then set history to 0.

3. Use **Buttons** as easy navigational tools; click on them instead of using the menu commands

4. **Error messages**

There will be instances where you are not able to access websites. You will get some kind of error message. The following are the most common problems and what to do about them:

a. Not getting link when you know the URL is correct>> Cutoff sections of address beginning with farthest right.

b. Busy signal on server>>Return later.

c. If nothing happens>>Click stop or refresh buttons.

d. URL changes>>Make best guess **or use a search tool.**

SEARCH TOOLS

There are many search tools, also called search engines, on the Web such as AltaVista, Lycos, Yahoo, Excite, and Google. The one search tool embedded in IE is MSN. You will see it when you hit the Search button. These tools are huge **databases** that are constantly updated and actively comb the Web for specific keyword(s). For example, typing AZ State Legislature or Navajo Nation in the search box. They are computer-generated and thus, will give you many "false drops" or sites that you discover are unrelated to your needs.

Go to your *Research Navigator Guide* (pages 9-13) for a more detailed discussion of this type of search tool.

There is a category of search tools that are called multiengines. They search using more than one tool or engine at a time and usually offer an integrated combination of the results. They are great time-savers. The best one of this type of search engine is called **Google**.

Make Google your default IE searcher.

The Google search tool is a useful, software utility that searches all of the major search engines. You can download it **free** and replace MSN in IE with it for a much more powerful search utility. It installs as its own toolbar under the address bar. Note that you can also find images, groups (Usenet discussion groups), a directory (a topical organization of websites) and the news (from over 4500 sources) on the Web using this tool

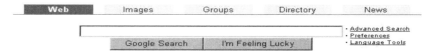

Here's How to Get Google:

1. Type *http://toolbar.google.com* in the browser's Address bar.

2. Click on the **Download Google Toolbar** button and click **open** in the download dialogue box.

3. Follow the series of instructions to complete the download.
   a. Welcome screen>>**agree**
   b. Choose your configuration>>**enable advanced features** and click next
   c. Final Instructions
      i. Select **google.com**
      ii. Click **Make Google my default search engine**
      iii. Click **Close all IE windows automatically**
      iv. Click next

4. The Google toolbar replaces IE's search button default (MSN or Dell) after installation. Now all searches will happen in Google. The Google Toolbar appears under your Address Bar. Clicking in the carrot next to search Web will change your search to images, groups, etc.

Practice: Exploring with Google.

1. Look in a category: type *child welfare policy*.

2. Find a name: type *who is Jane Addams*.

3. Search a geographical region for a topic: type *European approaches to adoption*.

4. Find images: type *Hispanic children* and make sure you select **Google Images** from dropdown menu.

5. Find an epilepsy support group: type *epilepsy support group* and make sure you select **Google Groups** from dropdown menu.

When you complete a search in Google, look to the right side of toolbar. It tells you how many hits on the subject it found and how long it took to find them. Scroll to bottom of page to view more sites.

Another type of search tool is huge **specialized directories,** also called **subject directories**, which are human run. They tend to eliminate the for-profit and trivial websites. These sites are most useful when you are looking at categories such as ethnic minorities, homelessness, and refugees.

An example of this type of search tool site for social work is World Wide Web Resources for Social Workers created and maintained by Dr. Gary Holden of NYU: *http://www.nyu.edu/socialwork/wwwrsw.* More social work sites of this type can be found in *Research Navigator Guide for the Helping Professions* (pages 132-136). Also go to pages 13-15 of this guide for more discussion on subject directories.

The third major search tool available to you is the **virtual library**. Almost every college and university have developed a website that serves as a gateway or bridge to the Internet and to other resources both within and outside the walls of the library building. For example, links exist to EJournals—online journals where you can read full text articles from professional journals. For many students and practitioners in remote sites access to a virtual library is an invaluable resource.

Practice: **Visit a university library.**
Go to *http://www.nau.edu/library* or your own college/university library website and explore the many avenues to resources. Take a virtual walk around the library without leaving your computer! Also, go glance over the virtual library sites in *Research Navigator Guide* (pages 15-16).

If it is really important, NEVER rely on only one search tool.

INTERNET SITES USEFUL IN SOCIAL WORK

The *Research Navigator Guide* contains hundreds of websites for you to use in your effective work with clients. They are divided into academic sites, government resources, professional association sites, electronic journals and newsletters, and an extensive listing of social work areas of practice sites (pages 136-246).

However, not all the sites you will visit, especially if you use the search engines that are not human run, will provide valid and reliable information. For many of these sites there are no filters on what is "garbage" and what is not. Your ability to identify the former from the latter is vitally important for effective client services.

WHAT MAKES FOR A LEGITIMATE WEBSITE?

Not all information you find on the Web is accurate, factual, or valid. If you are going to use information you find on the Web with clients, you ethically need to make sure that the information is valid. You also need to ensure the source material is trustworthy.

Imagine giving bogus information that you received from the Web to a client that was experiencing severe depression. This client could then use this information in a way that proved very harmful to them.

It is your responsibility as a competent social worker to be able to evaluate websites before sharing/using information with your clients.

Investigate issues such as:

- **Authority:** Who wrote the information? What are their credentials? Are they a qualified person on the subject? How do you find out? Is there an email address as minimal evidence?

- **Currency:** How up-to-date is the site? Are the links still working?

- **Domain:** Is it a for-profit parading as a non-profit? Does the domain match its purpose?

- **Coverage:** What is the breadth and depth of the site?

- **Accuracy:** Is the information factual, expert opinion or unsupported opinion?

To help you decide the answers to these questions and to help you decide the legitimacy of a site, go to the *Research Navigator Guide* (pages 16-23). Within these pages, you will find clear guidelines on how to evaluate a website so you are confident of its value in your professional practice.

THE CONVERGENCE OF THE INTERNET AND EVIDENCE-BASED PRACTICE

In teaching research to social work students, the link between research and practice is a "hard sell". Most social work research texts start off in their first chapter making the case for students to see themselves as research-practitioners: (Bisman & Hardcastle (1999); Rubin & Babbie (2001); Marlow (2001); Yegidis & Weinbach (2002); Neuman & Kreuger (2003); and Royse (2004). Yet, for many students who then become practitioners in agencies, their use of research to inform practice is resisted.

One of the major reasons given for this resistance is reported by Sheldon and Chilvers (2000). In their study, involving 1226 randomly selected, professional grade social care staff, over 80 percent of respondents reported that **lack of access to information** was a difficulty in their reading of and use of evaluative research to inform their practice.

In the past four years, the concept of evidence-based practice (EBP) has gained prominence in the field of social work: (Sheldon (2001); Taylor (2002); Marks (2002); Tierney (2002); Gibbs (2003); and Cournoyer (2004). Simply put, evidence-based practice combines searching the Internet to research practice related questions and applying the results to practice situations. While some might see it as a reworking of the research-practitioner linkage concept, EBP is becoming recognized as a necessary approach to practice that ensures effective client change and worker accountability. EBP uses research accessed from the Internet as a tool to inform competent practice.

Professor Stephanie Baus of Tulane University states the growth of EBP over the past five years coincides with the growth in the burgeoning numbers of online databases and other resources available to practitioners today. "Everyone is connected now; now is probably the first time social workers have been able to practice this type of methodology" (Marks (2002). p.10).

For more information on EPB see:

1. Centre for Evidence-Based Social Services
   - Site overview: *http://www.ex.ac.uk/cebss/*
   - Gateways typically contain research and reference information, and provide useful Web links. Usually these sites will have been developed by subject specialists so you can be fairly confident that they will hold relevant material and not too much nonsense. The number of online learning resources to help in evidence-based social care and health are growing rapidly. Interactive tutorials, e-libraries, networks, and discussion groups are just some examples of such resources.
   http://www.ex.ac.uk/cebss/gateways.html

2. Be Evidenced Based
   - The Be Evidence Based website is designed to provide easy access to key findings from critically appraised research in the field of social care.
   http://www.be-evidence-based.com/

3. SW Library at the University of Michigan School of Social Work: Secondary Data in Evidence-Based Practice
   http://www.lib.umich.edu/socwork/secondarydata.html

4. Web Resources for EPB
   http://www.columbia.edu/cu/musher/Web_sources_for_ebp.htm

5. Websites and Databases for EPB
   http://www.cf.ac.uk/socsi/rsu/issue3/Web.pdf

6. Evidence-Based Practice for the Helping Professions
   http://www.evidence.brookscole.com

ETHICAL ISSUES OF THE INTERNET AND IT

While the computer and the Internet are tremendous resources for you and your clients, these tools can also be the source of ethical violations and breaches of confidentiality. The emergence of many new technologies (computers, the Web, email, video-conferencing) becomes increasingly hampered by privacy concerns because these technologies leave our clients vulnerable to privacy abuses. The dilemma is letting clients choose between benefiting from the technology and maintaining privacy protections.

NASW (2003) makes a strong statement about these issues in its policy statement on technology and social work:

> Social workers must exercise careful judgment and take responsible steps to ensure the protection of clients' rights, respect for comfort level, and choice of technology use, confidentiality, and privacy when technology is used in practice.
>
> Social workers must inform their clients about the process, associated risks and benefits, and their rights and responsibilities when technology is used in practice (p. 339).[3]

---

[3] Policy statement approved by the NASW Delegate Assembly, August 1999. For further information, contact the National Association of Social Workers, 750 First Street, NE, Suite 700, Washington, DC 20002-4241. Telephone: 202-408-8600; email: press@naswdc.org.

Security and confidentiality

Earlier in this chapter, I spoke to you about Tools>>Internet Options>>Clear Temporary Files and Set History to 0. But, why? To illustrate the importance of these ethical practices, read the Clark case that follows. [4]

Clark

Clark killed himself after being confronted by his minister and three deacons in church over being gay. He was indeed gay, but far from ready to come out of his closet. Severely depressed, his exposure to the congregation and its "trial by gossip" was the final event in his tragic life. He was twenty-two.

The gossip had begun innocently enough. One of his other church members, a secretary at a local counseling center, had used the social worker's computer on her lunch break with the social worker's permission to explore the Web. This was just after the worker's session with Clark where they had spent an hour looking for gay lifestyle issues and resources on the Web. Clark had been really impressed with the resources that were available; they had found over ninety promising websites.

The secretary had been impressed too, because she reviewed Clark's complete session and immediately knew what Clark's issues were. She was a temporary worker and not been briefed in the agency's confidentiality policies or signed any agreements concerning information security. She just could not resist looking over what they had covered, and it had been so easy to follow the URLs and history that the computer had recorded.

When asked to recount the counseling session, the social worker stated: "We briefly discussed what resources might be found on the Web and then sat down at the computer for about an hour to look at websites. When we were done, I turned off the browser and we agreed on exploring various sites at the next opportunity. I then wrote my case summary on my computer and forwarded it to the central records file. Clark left the building and I took my lunch break."

---

[4] From Social Work and the Web 1st edition by Vernon/Lynch. ©2000. p. 52. Reprinted with permission of Wadsworth, a division of Thomson Learning: www.thomsonrights.com. Fax 800 730-2215.

This case is about a young man who commits suicide because he is outed due to the lack of computer security in an agency. If the temporary files had been cleared and the history set to 0 would Clark still be alive?

Unfortunately, Clark's case illustrates the more disturbing dimensions of the Web: passive breaches of confidentiality. Go to the NASW Code of Ethics on the NASW website: *http://www.socialworkers.org* and review Social Worker's Ethical Responsibility to Clients; specifically,

- 1.03 (e) Informed Consent
- 1.07 (l) Privacy and Confidentiality
- 1.07 (m) Privacy and Confidentiality

The emerging technology of telehealth

Alpine Community Mental Health Center is considering joining a consortium of agencies that is using telehealth to serve clients who are place-bound in the more rural parts of its catchment area. Northern Arizona Regional Behavioral Health Authority (NARBHA), the umbrella agency of this consortium, initiated this program in 1996 because of a shortage of qualified professionals to serve rural clients (Gibson, Morley, & Romeo-Wolff [2002]). This technology allows mental health professionals, including doctors, nurses, social workers, and others to see clients via video-conferencing for assessment and intervention without either worker or client having to drive hours for care.

Before we commit to be part of this group, many of our workers had ethical concerns about confidentiality, privacy, record-keeping, the impersonal interactions, client satisfaction, and interdisciplinary collaboration.

Sue Morley, NARBHA administrator of the telehealth program and a social worker, answered each of these concerns to our satisfaction via email communication during the week of September 22-26, 2003.

1. **Confidentiality and Privacy**: The site of the behavioral health care professional is careful to be sure that no one walks in the room when the client is being seen and the lines that carry the transmission are more secure than regular phone lines. We really work on helping the client feel more comfortable...having their case manager or therapist there

may help; others we let play with the remote control themselves and move the camera around; and of course we speak with them about the benefits/risks of telemedicine services, and talk with them about confidentiality issues. One of the protocols we do is to zoom the camera around, let the client see who is in the room, and tell them there will never be someone in the room that they are not notified of. Could there still be abuses? Of course. But that would be a major ethical violation that, if found, would be a serious offense for the professional.

2. **Record Keeping.** There are definitely new processes and procedures that are put in place to ensure the safety of medical records, since duplicate records are needed at the site where the medical practitioner is located. But none of these issues have been insurmountable.

3. **Impersonal Nature of Modality.** I think that many of the perceived hurdles about loss of personal connection are dealt with because of the large screen TV (28" or 32") and the focus of the person on the far end totally on the client. There really is face to face contact...its over video and in fact, you get a clearer, closer look at someone's face than in person. In fact, our staff say they can really look at someone longer and closer over video, than what is "socially appropriate" in person.

4. **Client Satisfaction.** For the first 3 years (and over 1000 clients) NARBHA required satisfaction survey's after every visit, from staff and clients. Clients were really complaining about the surveys, but loved the telemedicine.

5. **Interdisciplinary Collaboration.** It has also enhanced team efforts as the case manager or therapist is now more involved because they are present for most interactions with the psychiatrist.

For more information about the telehealth program at NARBHA, go to *http://narbha.org*. For more information about telehealth on the national scene, go to *http://tie.telemed.org*.

*We can be **no less** diligent in protecting the client's security and confidentiality issues on the computer, the Web, and other emerging technologies as we do with their paper files and records.*

Your Notes

Chapter 5
Spreadsheets and Agency Application

In this chapter, you will learn a variety of ways that a spreadsheet will be useful to you for agency and client work. Spreadsheets support accounting functions or any task that requires manipulation of numbers, such as asking for a salary increase! Plus, they are useful in producing charts—visual depictions of text and numbers. Utilize charts to accompany text in reports where you want to emphasize the data. Using Wizards, charts are easy to create. You'll see!

For our purposes, you will create a budget for Alpine Community Mental Health Center and show the cost trends via charts for the non-salary budget items of phone, travel, and supplies for the winter quarter of the year. Second, you will learn how to use formulas to quickly compute salary increases for staff and how much these increases will cost the agency. You will create a chart to display these increases. This task is called a "What If" scenario. Third, you will learn how to monitor and evaluate client progress by using single case designs and graphic visualization of client progress. You do not have to be a math whiz to do any of these tasks!

To accomplish these tasks, you will learn how to use:
- financial and data management functions, including autofill, calculations, autoformat, formatting cells and more
- chart creation and chart formatting tools
- formulas and charting for single case evaluations

Blank Workbook

A QUICK REVIEW OF A SPREADSHEET

1. As with every program in MS Office, first go to **Tools>>Options** to customize your Excel program. Review each tab and select those features that will make your work more efficient and easier.

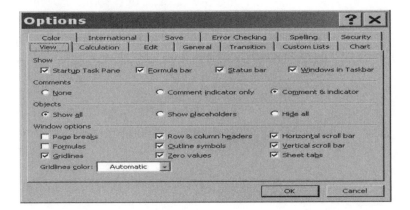

2. The term spreadsheet comes from ledger sheets—what accountants use to "spread" rows and columns of numbers out so their relationship can be seen visually. The advantage of computerized spreadsheets is that you can make changes without hand correcting large areas of ledger sheets. A change in one cell automatically changes the values in other cells when you use formulas.

3. Workbooks are files where you store worksheets. Workbooks/sheets in Excel are what Documents/pages are in Word.

   Because each workbook can contain many sheets, you can organize various kinds of related information in a single file. Worksheets are the individual pages within a workbook where data is entered and analyzed. Keep everything in one workbook. Worksheets are like chapters in a book.

4. Layout of a worksheet:
   a. Name box>>A1

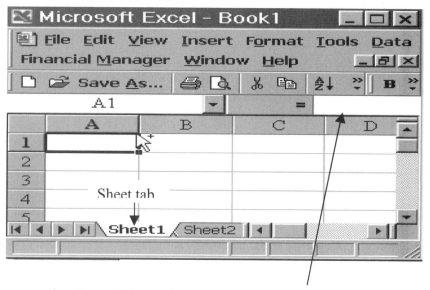

   b. Formula bar>>location to type formulas and other data
   c. Row headings>> 1-65,536
   d. Column headings>> A-IV (256 total)
   e. Sheet tabs: to be renamed to your needs (right click mouse)
      i. Default number of sheets is 3, but you can insert as many new worksheets as you want
      ii. Select **Insert>>Worksheet**
      iii. To delete a worksheet:
         1) Click on worksheet you want to delete
         2) **Edit>>Delete Sheet** or
            Right Click>>Delete

CREATING AN OPERATING BUDGET

1. In A1, type *Non-Salary Operating Budget* in 16 pt. and green. **Format>>Cells>>Font>>16 pt. and green.**

2. Save as *NonSalary Winter Budget 20041* in your ITSW folder.

3. In B3, type January. Grab handle in lower right corner of cell and drag across to March. This is called **Autofill.**

4. Beginning in **A4-A6**, type *Phone*, hit enter, *Travel*, enter, and *Supplies*.

5. Right click on Sheet 1 and rename *Winter 2004.*

6. Select row 2 and **Insert>>Row.**

7. Type *Total* in **E4** and **A8.**

8. Enter the data as follows:
   a. Phone—400, 350, 364 (tab, tab, tab, enter)
   b. Travel—800, 900, 700
   c. Supplies—250, 350, 325

9. To put $ sign in each cell at the same time, select B5-E8 and **Format>>Cells>>Number>>Currency>>Decimal Places: 0**

10. **Calculations**: To sum the rows and columns:
    a. Select E5 and select AutoSum icon on toolbar and hit enter
    b. Repeat this process for Travel and Supplies **or better yet**
    c. Grab handle in lower right of E5 and drag to E8
    d. Repeat entire process above at B8 for monthly totals
    e. Click on any box in the total row/column to note formula!

11. To give the budget a professional look, use **AutoFormat.**
    a. Select the data: A4-E8
    b. **Format>>AutoFormat>>Classic 1**

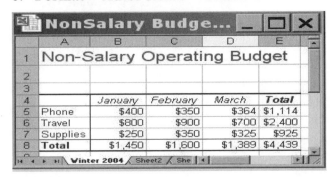

Chart-making of data

Visual representation of data allows you to see trends and patterns and, in the case of budgeting, permits you to estimate the budget needs for future quarters. Making charts is a 4-step process using the **Chart Wizard**. The Chart Wizard makes it easy to create and format charts and graphs. You will make separate charts for each budget item.

1. Select area you want to chart. In this case, select phone data: A5-D5 (not **total** cell: E5) and Select Chart Wizard.

2. Steps:
   a. Choose chart type: **Column—row 2, column1** (Clustered column with 3-D visual effect); **Press and Hold View Sample** to see what it looks like.

   b. Click Next and view data range information. This is what you highlighted on the spreadsheet.

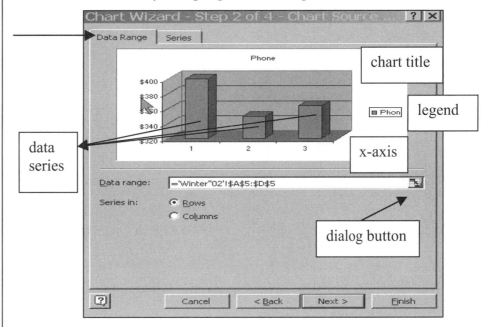

Data Range: ='Winter"02'!$A$5:$D$5. You read this formula; yes, it is a formula because it begins with an = sign as follows: the data in worksheet Winter'02 located in cells A5 to D5 is selected for the data range. The $ sign before the actual row and column locations locks in the cell data and makes that cell an *absolute* value. It cannot be changed.

i. Go to series tab to ensure months are visible; this is the x axis labels.

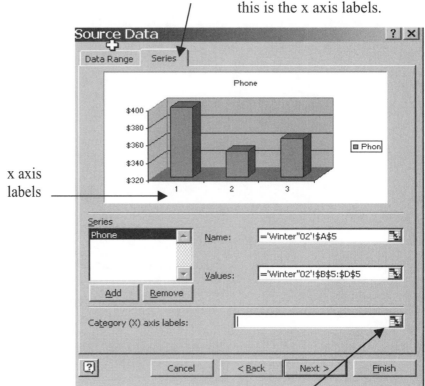

x axis labels

ii. If 1-3 is visible instead of the months, then click on dialog button. A smaller source data chart box appears. Select B4:D4 (months cells) and they will appear in this chart box. Close the box and the months now appear on the chart.

	A	B	C	D	E	F	G
1		Non-Salary Operating Budget					
2		Source Data - Category (X) axis labels:			? X		
3		='Winter"02'!$B$4:$D$4					
4		January	February	March	Total		
5	Phone	$400	$350	$364	$1,114		
6	Travel	$800	$900	$700	$2,400		
7	Supplies	$250	$350	$325	$925		
8	Total	$1,450	$1,600	$1,389	$4,439		

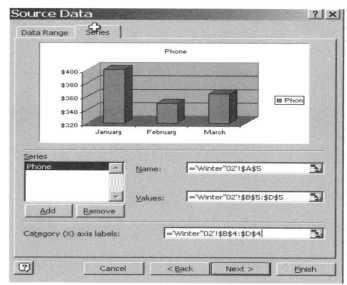

c. Click Next: **Chart Options** and modify as indicated below
   i. **Title:** Phone
   ii. **Axes:** Check both Category and Value
   iii. **Gridlines:** Set to your preferences; play
   iv. **Legend:** Deselect show legend
   v. **Data Labels:** Leave blank
   vi. **Data Table:** Leave blank

d. Click Next: **Chart Location**
   i. Click as **New Sheet>>***Winter Phone Chart*
   ii. Click **Finish**

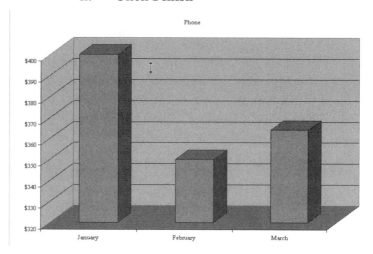

Practice: **Charts for travel and supplies.** Repeat chart creation procedure for the budget items *travel* and *supplies*. Click on **Winter 2004** tab to begin.

You can move the sheet tab: **Winter 2004** to beginning by selecting it, holding down the left mouse button, and moving the tab to the first position. You can move any tab to a new location this way.

3. As you can see, you can make charts of each individual item or combine them into **one chart for comparison**. To do the later:

   a. Select all three items with their corresponding data: A4-D7 and click on the chart icon and start the chart wizard.

   b. Choose Stacked column with a 3-D visual effect: Row 2: Column2>>next.

   c. Chart options:
      i. **Title:** *Non-Salary Items Comparison for Winter'04*
      ii. **Axes:** deselect Value (Z) axis
      iii. **Gridlines:** deselect Value (Z) axis major gridlines
      iv. **Legend:** select show legend
      v. **Data labels:** select show Value
      vi. **Data table:** none>>next

   d. Chart location: select as new sheet>>*Combined Items* and click finish.

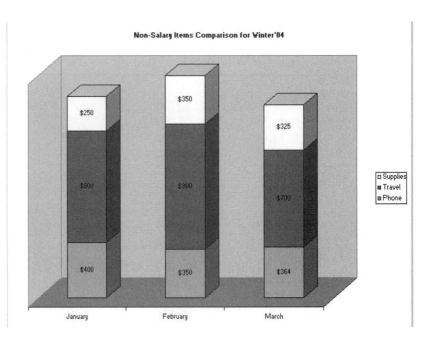

Enhancing your charts with custom formatting

You are able to change the shape, color, and size of any element on a chart. This is an area of creativity for you. Double click on any part of chart to bring up a dialogue box of choices for formatting or activate the **Chart Toolbar** from View>>Toolbars. If you move the pointer slowly over areas of the toolbar, you can see ToolTips identifying the items that make up the Chart toolbar.

Each item in the object list can be formatted separately.

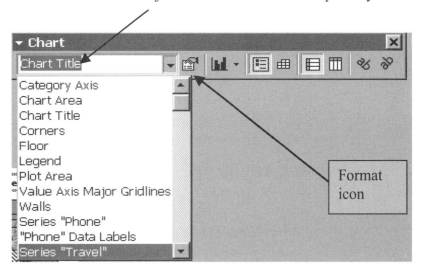

Experiment using your graphics skills! Try fill effects, color, font size...and more.

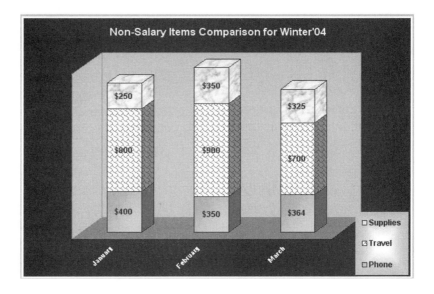

Close and save your file as *NonSalary Winter Budget 2004* to your ITSW folder.

"WHAT IF" SCENARIOS: ADVOCATING FOR PAY RAISE

By modifying factors related to a particular situation, a model or prediction is produced. Being able to model will enable you to plan for future programs, services, and/or staffing needs. For example, suppose your staff at Alpine Community Mental Health Center hasn't had a promised pay raise after being open nine months. You want a 3% increase. You know the board of directors is favoring only a 2% increase. Propose to them you want a 4% raise and then you can actually compromise on 3%.

By using Excel and yes, **formulas!**, you can demonstrate what the costs would be for each scenario. Here's how:

1. Open a new spreadsheet and at C1 type *Salary Projections* in 16 pt. bold.

2. Save as *Alpine Salary Projections1* in your ITSW folder.

3. Beginning in A3 enter the following labels in each successive cell across the row in 12 pt. bold and underline:
   Name, Position, Salary, 2%, 3%, and *4%.*

4. Format cells from C4 to F10 for currency:
   Format>>Cells>>Numbers>>Currency>>Decimals:0

5. Add data

Smith	Director	35000
Begay	Coordinator	29000
Jones	Coordinator	29000
Nez	Supervisor	25000
Lopez	Supervisor	25000
Rogers	Counselor	23500
Brown	Secretary	17000

Resizing columns—when the numbers in a column are wider than the width of the column, Excel fills the column with number signs (the # symbol) to let you know that there is a number in the cell, but it is too long to fit. By double-clicking on the right side column boundary line in the column header (where it says A or B, etc.), you can resize the column to fit the widest number in the column. This operation works with text columns as well when the text is cut off due to the width of the column.

6. How much is a 2% increase over current salary?
   a. Select D4 and in formula bar, type: =C4*102% (current salary plus 2% more).
   b. Hit return. Grab handle in lower right corner of D4 and pull down D column.
   c. **All formulas start with = sign.**

7. Repeat this process for 3% and 4%.

8. In B12, type *Total & Pay Raise* and in B13, type *Raise Cost;* align right in these cells.

9. **AutoSum** current salary in C12 and **Fill Right** for increases.

10. In D13, calculate the cost difference between total raise increase and total current salary by subtracting the current salary from the increase: Enter =*D12-$C$12* in formula bar, where **$C$12** is an absolute cell value. (This value is used in all three scenarios; see glossary for description of absolute cell value). **Fill Right**.

		Salary Projections			
Name	**Position**	**Salary**	**2%**	**3%**	**4%**
Smith	Director	$35,000	$35,700	$36,050	$36,400
Begay	Coordinator	$29,000	$29,580	$29,870	$30,160
Jones	Coordinator	$29,000	$29,580	$29,870	$30,160
Nez	Supervisor	$25,000	$25,500	$25,750	$26,000
Lopez	Supervisor	$25,000	$25,500	$25,750	$26,000
Rogers	Counselor	$23,500	$23,970	$24,205	$24,440
Brown	Secretary	$17,000	$17,340	$17,510	$17,680
	Total & Pay Raise	$183,500	$187,170	$189,005	$190,840
	Raise Cost		$3,670	$5,505	$7,340

11. Enhance the look of the chart. Select A1:F13. **Format>>Autoformat>>List 3**.

12. Rename sheet1 tab: *Salary Projections*

13. **Make a Chart of 3% Increase**.

The choice of chart type is very much influenced by what it is you want to portray. In this case, a pie chart would be most appropriate as it gives the percentage of total salary for each position and demonstrates a fairly equitable distribution of funds.

a. Select E4:E10 and open Chart Wizard.

b. Select **Pie Chart>>Row 1: Column 1.**

c. Click Next and tab to series;
   i. type *3% Salary Increase Distribution* after name
   ii. click on category labels and highlight the positions. Click next.

d. Chart Options>>Data Labels>>Show percent & legend key next to label; click next

e. Select as new sheet and name it *Pie Distribution*

f. Format as follows: (open Chart toolbar or double click in each chart area)
   i. **Chart Title:** 18 pt. bold and move closer to pie.
   ii. **Chart Area:** Patterns>>Light Grey>>Fill Effects>>One Color.
   iii. **Legend:** same pattern procedure as Chart Area.
   iv. **Data Labels:** Font>>16 pt. and bold.

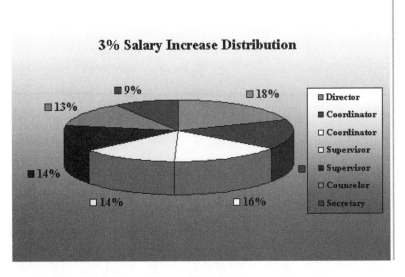

14. It would cost the Board only **$1835** ($5505-$3670) more than they planned to make the staff happy. Advocate for your staff!

15. Keep file open.

Excel Printing

You probably waste a lot of time and paper sending entire worksheets to the printer when all you need is a printout of a few columns or rows. Here's how:

1. Select **View>>Page Break Preview**

2. Select the cells you want to print.

		Salary Projections			
Name	**Position**	**Salary**	**2%**	**3%**	**4%**
Smith	Director	$35,000	$35,700	$36,050	$36,400
Begay	Coordinator	$29,000	$29,580	$29,870	$30,160
Jones	Coordinator	$29,000	$29,580	$29,870	$30,160
Nez	Supervisor	$25,000	$25,500	$25,750	$26,000
Lopez	Supervisor	$25,000	$25,500	$25,750	$26,000
Rogers	Counselor	$23,500	$23,970	$24,205	$24,440
Brown	Secretary	$17,000	$17,340	$17,510	$17,680
Total & Pay Raise		$183,500	$187,170	$189,005	$190,840
Raise Cost			$3,670	$5,505	$7,340

3. Right click on the selection and choose **Set Print Area** from the shortcut menu.

4. **File>>Print>>Print what>>Selection>>Preview.**

5. Select **Setup>>**
   a. **Header/Footer>>Header>>Custom Header>>Left Section>>** A in 12 pt. bold: *Cost Projections*

   b. **Sheet>>Print Gridlines.**
   c. The result to be printed:

Cost Projections

Total & Pay Raise	$183,500	$187,170	$189,005	$190,840
Raise Cost		$3,670	$5,505	$7,340

6. **Print…**

7. **View>>Normal.**

8. Close file to ITSW folder.

EVALUATING CLIENT PROGRESS

Single case designs provide you with a systematic, valid, and empirical way to evaluate what you do with clients.

- It provides continuous feedback which allows for treatment change during, not after, treatment is complete.
- It identifies the point when change occurs and in what behaviors and how long lasting the change is.
- It reduces subjectivity and opinion of the worker during the evaluation of treatment.
- It supports the social work value of mutuality and empowers clients because they are intimately involved in their own evaluation.

In short, single case design is directly related to the effectiveness of what you do with clients (Rubin & Babbie [2001]).

You will demonstrate evaluation in direct practice using a single case design with Mrs. Smith, whom you are seeing for depression. With the computer you are able to depict visual presentation of clinical data for both yourself and the client system. Single case designs show continuous measurement of target behaviors during baseline, intervention, and second baseline periods. Here's how:

1. Open a new spreadsheet document, save to your ITSW folder and title it *Smith Evaluation Practice1*. Make sure default font is Times New Roman in 12 pt.

2. Rename sheet 1 as *Smith Progress*.

3. Make a title for your client system's progress as follows: *Single Case Design for Client System Smith: Depression* in capital letters, bold, beginning in A1.

4. The labels are to be called *INDICATORS* and *DAY*. Type these labels in bold, centered in C3 and in A5, respectively. (Double click on right column line of C to expand to fit text.)

5. The behaviors that you will be measuring are: *hrs. of sleep/day; no. of calls to sn (social network)/day ; and felt like crying/day.*
   a. Center, bold, no caps, and type them is B4, C4, and D4, respectively (again, double click on columns to expand them to fit text).

b. Bold and type days *1-22* beginning in A6.

Type *1* and *2* to start pattern, select both cells, and grab the handle in lower right corner and drag to 22

6. ENTER THE FOLLOWING DATA:

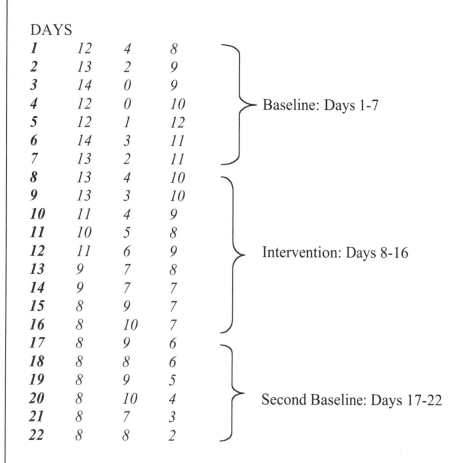

DAYS

1	*12*	*4*	*8*	
2	*13*	*2*	*9*	
3	*14*	*0*	*9*	
4	*12*	*0*	*10*	Baseline: Days 1-7
5	*12*	*1*	*12*	
6	*14*	*3*	*11*	
7	*13*	*2*	*11*	
8	*13*	*4*	*10*	
9	*13*	*3*	*10*	
10	*11*	*4*	*9*	
11	*10*	*5*	*8*	
12	*11*	*6*	*9*	Intervention: Days 8-16
13	*9*	*7*	*8*	
14	*9*	*7*	*7*	
15	*8*	*9*	*7*	
16	*8*	*10*	*7*	
17	*8*	*9*	*6*	
18	*8*	*8*	*6*	
19	*8*	*9*	*5*	
20	*8*	*10*	*4*	Second Baseline: Days 17-22
21	*8*	*7*	*3*	
22	*8*	*8*	*2*	

7. Separate each of the measurement periods:

a. Put an underline at day 7 and day 16.
   1) Select each row
   2) Click on bottom line in borders

b. Color baseline data in **blue**, intervention data in **green**, and second baseline in **red** (do not select DAYS column, only the data). How?
   1) Select each section
   2) **Format>>Cells>>Color>>Select the color>>**Click OK

c. Add comment to day 7: *end of baseline* and day 16: *end of intervention using reality therapy.*

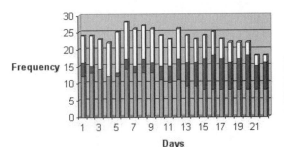

1) Select each designated day
2) **Insert>>Comment>>type info above.**
3) **View>>Comments** to close them.
4) Move cursor over red mark in these days and comments appear.

8. **Chart Making for All Behaviors**

Visual depiction of client progress provides instant feedback to the client and you as well as serves as a reinforcer of positive behavior. These charts are powerful tools in client evaluation.

a. Rename sheet 2 as *Smith Charts*
b. Select all client data **(B6:D27)** from Smith Progress.
c. Click on **Chart Wizard icon.** Select column chart: row 2, column 2 (a **stacked column with a 3-D effect)** for all three indicators. Press preview. Click next.
d. Go to **series** tab:
  i. Select **series 1:** Name>>*hrs. of sleep/day*
  ii. Select **series 2:** Name>>*no. of calls to sn/day*
  iii. Select **series 3:** Name>>*felt like crying/day* Click next.
e. **Chart title:** *Smith Progress: Depression*
f. **Category (x axis):** *Days*
g. **Value (z) axis:** *Frequency*
h. **Legend:** check show legend, placement to right. Click next.
i. **As object in:** *Smith Charts* (click down carrot).

Smith Progress: Depression

9. **Chart Formatting of All Behaviors: Let's Make It Shine!**
   a. Resize to fit so that all data is showing
   b. Format Days and Frequency to 14 pt., Legend to 14 pt., and Title to 18 pt.
   c. Align frequency to 90 degrees
   d. Format Chart area to shadow, rounded corners, and color light gray
   e. Format Legend area to same light gray and remove border line

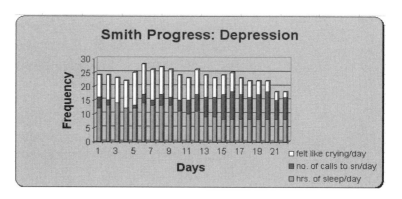

10. **Chart Making and Formatting for Each Behavior**
   a. Make a **line** chart (row 2: column 1) for each separate indicator on Smith Progress
   b. Title each chart with appropriate indicator
   c. Remove gridlines and uncheck show legend
   d. Place on Smith Charts below previous chart

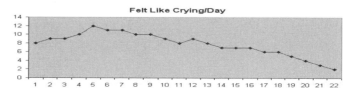

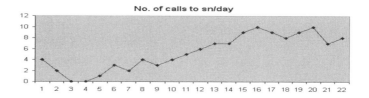

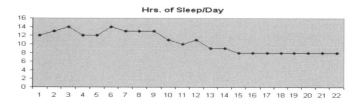

Being able to show your clients the changes in their behavior visually is both reinforcing and empowering to them.

Is the client change significant?

Visual significance is only one way to ascertain whether intervention is effective and termination is in order. **Practical significance** answers the question whether the amount of change is important from a clinical standpoint. For example, does the reduction of fire setting from ten times per week to two times per week for a pyromaniac warrant a significant enough change for termination? Sometimes visual and/or practical significance is not enough to make this determination.

Statistical significance[1] may be necessary. In order to run tests of significance (*T or F tests*) on this data (you will not be required to do this now), you need to find the averages of each variable in each measurement period.

11. Copy and paste labels and data from Smith Progress sheet: **A3:D27** onto sheet 3 and rename sheet *Smith Stats* (again, click on right column line to resize each column).

12. Put an additional row after days 7 and 16. Click on #11 in grey column to far left and then **Insert>>Row**. Repeat procedure on #21.

13. Type in the word **Average** in column A of these rows and after the last row of data.

14. Compute and insert the averages for each of the three behaviors at each measurement period. Make **number** at two decimal points.
     a. Select B11.
     b. Put =sign in formula bar.
     c. Select **Average** from Type menu and double click on it.
     d. Make sure range is **B4:B10,** click OK and **Fill Right.**

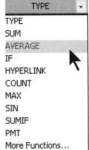

---

[1] A limitation of statistical significance in single-case designs is the small number of data points (measurement) in these designs. This can lead to results that are not statistically significant. Rubin and Babbie (2001) state "you should be careful not to let the lack of statistical significance carry too much weight when you interpret findings that are visually or practically significant (p. 689).

e. Repeat procedure for intervention average, **B12:B20** and for second baseline average, **B22:B27.**

15. Format each of these average rows in black and bold.

	A	B	C	D
1			INDICATORS	
2		hrs. of sleep/day	no. of calls to sn/day	felt like crying/day
3	DAY			
4	1	12	4	8
5	2	13	2	9
6	3	14	0	9
7	4	12	0	10
8	5	12	1	12
9	6	14	3	11
10	7	13	2	11
11	Average	12.86	1.71	10.00
12	8	13	4	10
13	9	13	3	10
14	10	11	4	9
15	11	10	5	8
16	12	11	6	9
17	13	9	7	8
18	14	9	7	7
19	15	8	9	7
20	16	8	10	7
21	Average	10.22	6.11	8.33
22	17	8	9	6
23	18	8	8	6
24	19	8	9	5
25	20	8	10	4
26	21	8	7	3
27	22	8	8	2
28	Average	8.00	8.50	4.33

16. Save your work in your ITSW folder.

SUMMARY

The spreadsheet application has much more utility to you than just keeping budgets. With the ability to model, you are able to accurately plan for future growth in programs, services, and staffing needs in your agency. You are also able to work with your client systems in their process of change and show them visual representation of their progress. Using charts creates immediate and positive feedback for clients as well as offers visual depiction of data to agency personnel, community members, and reporting sources.

I told you that you didn't have to be a math whiz!

Your Notes

Chapter 6
Databases and Agency Application

Databases are list management programs in which you can organize, sort, and analyze data in a number of ways. You can create forms, filter information, make reports, and use mail merge with a Word document for individualized and personalized form letters. The database program Access, in MS Office, is probably the most powerful of all the Office programs you will use.

Given the lack of centralized services as found in urban centers, rural social service agencies do not generally have access to a book of information and referral resources. Smaller cities, like Flagstaff, AZ, have a directory that is compiled by a volunteer organization such as the Assistance League, but it covers only the city area, not the surrounding rural communities and is published once a year.

Often times workers in rural agencies have a personalized list of names and numbers that they keep; some on torn papers; some on business cards; some in address books. In other words, it's a mess!

The ability to retrieve a needed service for a client is just good practice. In this chapter, you will learn how to:
- create a computerized database (an information and referral directory) of area agencies.
- manipulate the data in this directory in order to sort these agencies by specific criteria such as city or kind of service.
- generate a hard copy report of any part of the directory to give to clients.
- utilize the mail merge function to send individualized letters to agencies for updating their information using a single form letter for all of them.

A QUICK REVIEW OF ACCESS DATABASE BASICS

1. To open a new database, click the blank Access database icon in New Office Document from the Start menu.

Blank Database

2. You have to give the file a name immediately before you can even begin work in the database. You will call the file: *Alpine IR Directory1*, save it to your **ITSW** folder and then click create.

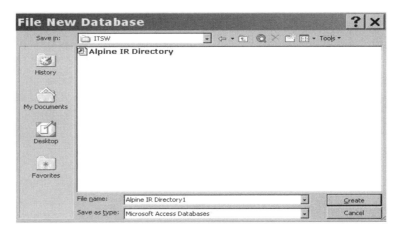

3. As you can see from the screen, there are three ways to create a table. A table is actually a file like in Word. However this file or table contains records (all the information you decide you want about a person or item; in this case it will be an agency). Each bit of information within the record is called a field.

a. **Create table in Design view** is the best way to create your database. While it takes some forethought and upfront time, it will be the most productive and useful way to begin your database.
b. **Create table by using a wizard** allows you to select predetermined fields that correspond to mainly business world tasks such as products and orders. This is not useful for us.
c. **Create table by entering data** allows you to enter information in fields, but is not the most efficient as you need to go back and designate field names for these data.

4. The **objects box** (to the left of the create choices) provides different ways to manipulate your data once you have entered it into the table. You will be introduced to queries, forms, and reports a little later.

5. Finally, as in Word and Excel, review the choices you have to customize Access by going to **Tools>>Options**.

CREATING ALPINE INFORMATION AND REFERRAL (I&R) DIRECTORY

1. Think about what info (fields) you want your records on referral agencies to contain before creating the table. You can always add/delete fields afterwards, but it saves time to plan ahead. Each bit of text is its own field. For example, street address, city, state, and zip are separate fields. Making the fields individualized will allow you to sort and filter by specific criteria such as city or zip.

2. Open Access by clicking on **create table in Design view.** Your window requires you to add Field Name, Data Type (what kind of data in the field), and Field Properties (your ability to customize the field). When you click in a box, there is a description of what that box does.

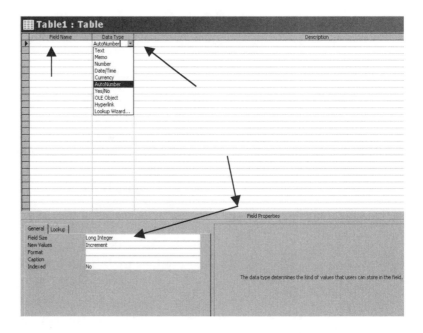

3. Add the following information into the table:

Field Name	Data Type	Field Properties
ID#	auto#	yes (no duplicates)
Update	date	format>short date
Agency	text	field size> 75
Street	text	
City	text	
State	text	field size> 2; default value>AZ
Zip	text	field size> 5 input mask> 00000
Phone	text	input mask> (999) 000-0000
Fax	text	input mask> (999) 000-0000
Contact fName	text	
Contact lName	text	
Service 1	Lookup Wizard>>see #4	
Service 2	Lookup Wizard>>see #4	

Press F1 for help on options available in any of the field property choices.

4. Data Type: **Lookup Wizard>> Select "I will type..."** Click next.

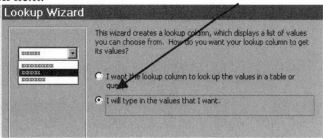

5. Select **Columns=1** and tab to add services. Click next.

> Counseling-MH
> Counseling-SA
> Counseling-Family
> Elderly-home care
> Elderly-case management
> Housing
> Support Groups
> Other

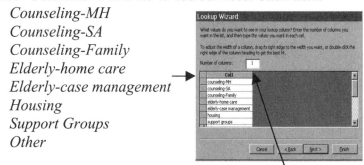

If data extends beyond the space allotted, then double click on column edge

6. **Label**>>*Service 1*; repeat for *Service 2* with same service listings as above.

7. Close and *save as* in table name box: *IR Agencies* and say **yes** to primary key when its window appears.

8. Click on IR agencies from Tables Object Box and scroll across to Service 1 and pull down the carrot to see how the lookup function works.

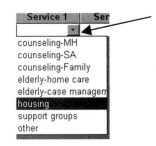

9. **Data Entry:**
   a. You can add data directly into the table by typing the info into each field and tabbing across the fields
   b. **or** you can create a form to enter it—the easier way; entering data on the form automatically puts the same data in the table.

10. **Forms**>>**Create form by using Wizard**
    a. **Objects box**>> Form
    b. **Name of Table**>> IR Agencies
    c. **Select Fields**>> All (the double >>)
    d. **Layout Choice**>>Justified
    e. **Background Style**>>Blends
    f. **Name**>> *Alpine Agency Listings*>>Finish
    g. Open Form

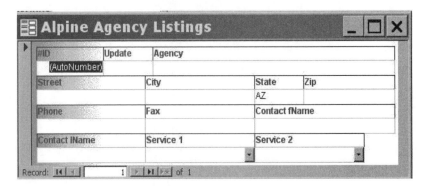

11. To save time with the data entry of agencies, close this file without saving. Go to the files in your ITSW Folder. Open *Alpine IR Directory* file. Go to **Objects Box**>>**Forms**>>Alpine Agency Listings.

12. Add another agency's info as record #6 for practice and close the forms box.

Please note the following as a result of how you designed the table:
   a. In the ID# field, the number is automatically inserted once you hit enter.
   b. The date field will display the short date style even if you type out the month, day, year.
   c. In the state box, AZ is already added as default value.
   d. In the phone and fax boxes, note that you only have to input the numbers as the shell is already created.
   e. The drop down choices are available for services1 and 2.

DATA MANIPULATION

Consider that your I&R Directory has grown to over 100 agencies. How do you quickly find specific information that you want in the database?

Select table in the objects box and open IR Agencies:

Sort: Use icon [icon] or Records>>Sort; remember to select the field you want to sort first.

Practice: Sort by City.
   a. Highlight city field
   b. Click on sort AZ∃

Agency	Street	City
VICTIM WITNESS SERVICES OF COCONINO COUNTY	11 Leroux Street	Flagstaff
NACA	2717 N. Steves Blvd.	Flagstaff
PARENTS ANONYMOUS OF NA	301 N. West St.	Flagstaff
GUIDANCE CENTER AT GRAND CANYON	3 Rim Drive	Grand Canyon
CC COMMUNITY SERVICES	14 Flower St.	Williams

Find Use icon 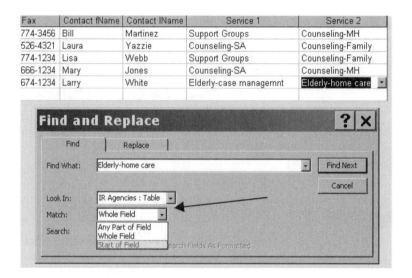 or **Edit>>Find**; finds one piece of data of interest

Practice: **Find all agencies providing elderly-home care services.**

Make sure you select the match type you want. In this case
it is the **whole field**.

The **Find** function can only select **one** record at a time. If you want
a listing of all agencies providing this service than use the **Filter**
function.

Filters Finds and selects **all** data of specific interest

1. **Filter by selection**

    Can only select criteria in **one** field of table

    Practice: Find all Flagstaff agencies.

    a. Double-click on Flagstaff in one record
    b. Click on **Filter by selection** icon

IR Agencies : Table

#ID	Update	Agency	Street	City	State
1	9/30/2004	PARENTS ANC	301 N. West St	Flagstaff	AZ
2	12/2/2004	NACA	2717 N. Steves	Flagstaff	AZ
5	6/24/2004	VICTIM WITNE!	11 Leroux Stree	Flagstaff	AZ

c. Click on Funnel (remove filter) to return to full list

2. **Filter by form**

Can select criteria in **multiple** fields

Practice: **Find all Flagstaff agencies who do counseling-Family or counseling-SA.**

a. Click the **filter by form** icon
b. Click on City and select Flagstaff from drop down box in one record
c. Select Counseling-SA in service 1 **or** Counseling-Family in service 2 by clicking on *or* at bottom of screen for each service field

Look for　　　Or

d. Click on Funnel (apply filter)

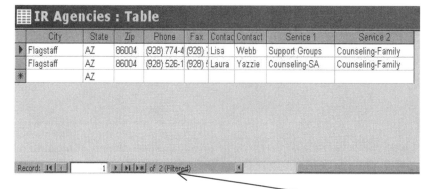

IR Agencies : Table

City	State	Zip	Phone	Fax	Contad	Contact	Service 1	Service 2
Flagstaff	AZ	86004	(928) 774-4	(928) :	Lisa	Webb	Support Groups	Counseling-Family
Flagstaff	AZ	86004	(928) 526-1	(928) :	Laura	Yazzie	Counseling-SA	Counseling-Family
*	AZ							

Record: 1 of 2 (Filtered)

e. Note that there are two records that match this filter.

QUERIES   Queries locate specific information according to special criteria; they answer specific questions. They are more powerful than filters in that they can isolate a group of records **plus limit the fields to be included.**

Practice: Before September'04 Phone Update.
You want to keep your I&R directory current. You have not updated since September, 2004. You need to identify all the agencies with Update field date before September 1, 2004.

1. In Objects box, select **Query** and choose **Create query by using wizard**

2. Make sure you choose **Table: IR Agencies** from pull down menu

3. Select the following fields: update, agency, phone, contact fname, contact lname. Click next.

4. Title query *Before September'04 Phone Update1* **and**

5. Select **modify the query design butto**n. Click finish.

6. In criteria box of update field, type *<09/01/04*

7. Hit Run Icon

> **some criteria values**
> < is less than
> > is greater than
> = is equal to
> **not** is excluding a characteristic; ex: **not** Flagstaff

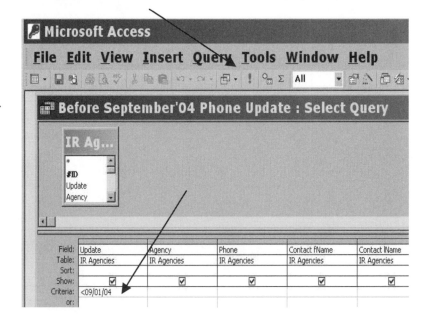

- 92 -

Before September'04 Phone Update : Select Query

Update	Agency	Phone	Contact fName	Contact lName
1/9/2004	CC COMMUNIT	(928) 674-4321	Larry	White
6/24/2004	VICTIM WITNES	(928) 774-6543	Bill	Martinez

8. Two agencies need to be called. You now have all the information to contact these agencies by phone to update their information. Close and click save.

Practice: Before September'04 Mail Update.

Let's say you know that there are too many agencies that need updating and that phoning each one would take too much time. You need to send a letter to each agency with their agency information enclosed (from **report** file that you will create in the next section) asking them to update any changes and send the updated sheet back to you. You will type a form letter that will be personalized to every agency (**mail merge**) using the data that you will now create in the query, *Before September'04 Mail Update 1.*

1. In the Objects box, select **Queries** and choose **Create query by using wizard.**

2. Make sure you choose **Table: IR Agencies** from pull down menu **and not** Query: Before September'04 Phone Update **or** Query: Before September'04 Phone Update1.

3. Select the following fields: update, agency, street, city, state, zip, contact fname and contact lname >> next

4. Title query *Before September'04 Mail Update1* **and**

5. Select **modify the query design button**. Click finish.

6. In criteria box of update field, type *<09/01/04*

7. Hit Run Icon

8. The result: 2 agencies will receive personalized form letters.

Before September'04 Mail Update : Select Query

Update	Agency	Street	City	State	Zip	Contact fName	Contact lName
1/9/2004	CC COMMUNIT	14 Flower St.	Williams	AZ	86534	Larry	White
6/24/2004	VICTIM WITNES	11 Leroux Stree	Flagstaff	AZ	86001	Bill	Martinez

9. Close and click save.

REPORTS

Reports can give you a customized version of your data wherein you can insert pictures, headers/footers, page numbers and more. You might want a hardcopy of your Information and Referral Directory or be able to give a copy of an agency's info to a client.

1. Select **Reports** from Objects Box and click on **Create report by using wizard**

2. Select the correct table to use in the report. **Table: IR Agencies**

3. **Select all >>** and move back ID# and Update. Click next.

4. **No** to grouping levels. Click next.

5. Sort by **Agency**. Click next.

6. Layout is **Columnar**; orientation is **Portrait.** Click next.

7. Style is **Bold**. Click next.

8. Title: *Alpine CMHC Information and Referral Directory1* **and**

9. Click on **Modify the report's design** and then click next.

10. A design view with several sections appears.

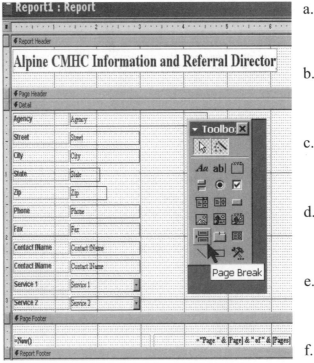

a. Report header

b. Page header

c. Detail

d. Page footer

e. Report footer

f. Toolbox

11. To customize the report, do the following:

    a. Click on **page break icon** in toolbox and insert a page break at end of service 2 so that each agency is on a separate page.

    b. Put cursor on top line of detail bar (just below page header bar). It changes to a **crosshair**. Move detail bar down about 1.5".

    c. Move **Alpine CMHC Information and Referral Directory** from report header area to page header area and resize it by clicking on it to look like this image.

        Alpine CMHC Information and Referral Directory

    d. Move this title so that it begins at the 2" horizontal ruler. Put cursor on top line of page header bar; the arrow turns into a crosshair. Move the bar up to the bottom of the report header bar.

    e. In page header area, insert agency logo from agency letterhead template and place to left of title. Click on **unbound object frame icon** in toolbox and move logo into place.

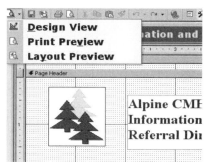

    f. Put your cursor on top line of detail bar; the arrow turns to a crosshair and moves the bar down .5". This will give space between the title & image and agency data.

    g. Go to view button in upper left to toggle between design and print view to preview how your report will look. Make any adjustments you wish.

h. The report result:

Alpine CMHC Information and Referral Directory

Agency	Coconino County Community Services
Street	14 Flower St.
City	Williams
State	AZ
Zip	86534
Phone	(928)674-4321
Fax	(928)674-1234
Contact fName	Larry
Contact lName	White
Service 1	Elderly-case management
Service 2	Elderly-home care

Wednesday, October 08, 2003   Page 1 of 6

➤ Each agency and all of its data are on a separate page.

➤ Each page has the date and page number.

➤ The agencies are in alphabetical order.

➤ You can print any page separately to give to a client.

12. Close database.

MAIL MERGE TO SEND FORM LETTERS

If you have many agencies that are in your I&R directory, you might want to send these agencies update forms instead of calling them. You can create a form letter that is personalized with names, addresses, and other specific data from your database of agencies. You combine the variable information with the form letter text and each recipient gets a personalized letter. You can do this very quickly by using the **mail merge** function.

Creating a form letter is a simple **6-step process** using the mail merge wizard. As you type the text for your form letter, you insert merge fields for each record's information. Then you merge (input) the actual database information with the letter's text to create your personalized letter. You must have created and saved information in your database before beginning this operation. You already did this.

1. Open a new Word document and choose **Tools>>Letters and Mailing>>Mail Merge Wizard.**

2. Select document type as **Start from template>>select template** and click the general tab to find your agency template that you created.

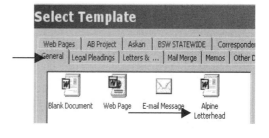

3. Select recipients. You will browse to your ITSW folder and open your Alpine IR Directory file and click open. A dialogue box will open with your choices of tables. Select **Before September'04 Mail Update** and click OK.

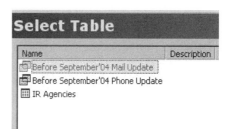

4. Begin writing your letter. Insert date, then hit enter four times, click address block, make sure all boxes are checked, and choose the recipient's first and last name without a salutation.

a. Click on Match Fields and make necessary changes:

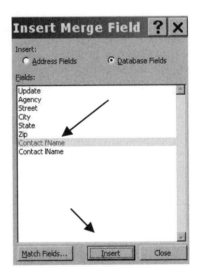

1. contact lname for last name

2. contact fname for first name

3. agency for company

4. street for address1

b. Double space and type *Dear*, click on more items and select **Contact fname**, click **insert** and close. Put a comma after it, and double space.

c. Type *It has been since* [click more items... and **select update field** and close] *that we have information about your agency...*

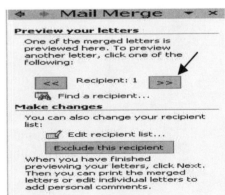

5. Preview your letters: there should be two to view.

6. Completing the merge is the last step. Cancel print as you will not need to do this now.

The Result:

Inserting merge data

Alpine Community Mental Health Center
linking people with the resources they need

123 Leroux St. Flagstaff, AZ 86001
(928) 774-1234 (928)774-4321 (fax)
www.aplinecmhc.org

October 8, 2004

««AddressBlock»»

Dear «Contact_fName»,

It has been since «Update» that we have information about your agency....|

Completing the merge

Alpine Community Mental Health Center
linking people with the resources they need

123 Leroux St. Flagstaff, AZ 86001
(928) 774-1234 (928)774-4321 (fax)
www.aplinecmhc.org

October 8, 2004

Larry White
Coconino County Community Services
14 Flower St.
Williams, AZ 86534

Dear Larry,

It has been since 1/9/2004 that we have information about your agency....|

If you have any problems with the mail merge—either while you are using the Mail Merge Wizard or afterward—get help. Click on Office Assistant under the Help menu, type *mail merge* and click on the problem that applies.

TOURO COLLEGE LIBRARY

SUMMARY

As you can see, Access is the most powerful of all the Office programs. It is not easy to learn initially, as there are many different operations it can perform. Once you have mastered these operations, however, you will be able to maintain the most current information in your databases and manipulate these data in a multitude of ways—sorting, filtering, querying, merging, and more.

The best way to feel competent using Access in your work is to practice. There are assignments you will be asked to do that create a client database and a board of directors database for Alpine Community Mental Health Center. Be patient with yourself in these exercises; it is worth it!

TOURO COLLEGE LIBRARY

Chapter 7
Slide Shows and Agency Application

PowerPoint (PP) is a presentation graphics program designed to add visual appeal to your public talks. It produces full color slides in which you can easily enter text, images, pictures, charts, and animation. The animated presentations include transition effects between slides and sophisticated animation on individual slides. Even charts can be animated. Slide shows can also contain video, audio clips, music, and narration though you need high-end computers to handle these effects. You can still knock peoples' socks off without these extras which can be distracting.

You need a computer (preferably a notebook type), your PP presentation on disk as well as loaded on the computer (for backup purposes) and a large screen (no smaller than 40") and a LCD projector. Public talks are more engaging when your audience can view visuals as well as listen to you. It is also important that they are provided with a handout of your talk on which they may take notes and comments.

In this chapter, you will create an Annual Agency Report in PP consisting of eight slides to present to the Alpine Community Mental Health Center Board of Directors. You will incorporate many of the skills learned in earlier chapters. You will input information from some of the files that you've already produced.

In addition, you will learn some new skills. They include:

- How to build your annual report through slide selection, template design, color schemes, chart creation, and copy/paste text and pictures from other files.

- How to animate your slide show using visual transitions between slides and text and chart transitions in slides.

- How to display and print your slide show including rehearsing the delivery, using aids in the shows, and choosing various print options.

REVIEWING THE BASICS

Before you learn to copy, edit, format, create objects, pictures, charts, and text into a presentation for the board, let's go over some basics:

1. Plan ahead on paper:
    a. What you want to say. Remember the slide content ought to be in **short bullets**; your accompanying talk will fill in the fine points.
    b. Create a detailed outline of the content you to say, including presentation goal, key points, sub points, and supporting information.
    c. Decide on visual content you want to include: images, pictures, charts, etc.

2. PowerPoint Rules:
    a. Font size of text should be no smaller than 24 pt.
    b. There should be no more than six major lines of text per slide.
    c. For your audience to be able to read the text there must be enough color contrast between the background and the text colors.
    d. Don't jam the slides full of text and then read it to your audience.

3. Open new PowerPoint document.

4. A new window screen appears that contains several parts. This is the normal view of a window. Let's go over them.

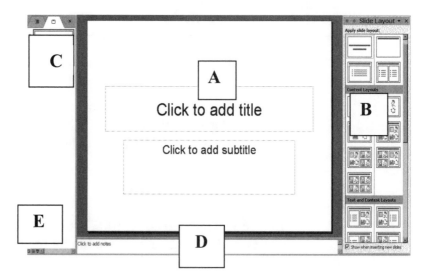

5. There are five panes on your screen.
   a. **Slide pane:** displays the current slide. When you first open a presentation, it always defaults to the title slide.
   b. **Task Pane:** offers you a shortcut to the most common tasks in PP, including slide layout, slide design, custom animation, slide transitions.
   c. **Outline/slide pane toggle:** displays text on each slide. You can also add text to slides from the outline view.
   d. **Notes pane:** your speaker notes which are seen only by you when you select this option for printing.
   e. **Shortcut bar:** in lower left where you can toggle to:
      i. Normal view which is the default you now see.
      ii. Slide sorter view which shows all slides created. This view is helpful to reorder, move, or cut slides.
      iii. Slideshow view which activates the presentation mode.

6. The menu bar displays the commands available in PP. As in every program in Office, customize your PP. **Tools>>Options** and make your changes. Clicking on the **New Slide** button changes the task pane to **Slide Layout** where you then choose the type of slide you want.

7. Click on **Slide Design** button and the task pane changes:
   a. Click **Design Template**—choosing a consistent background for your slides. Scroll down until you find a design called **Capsules.** Click on the carrot next to the slide and choose **Apply to all slides.**
   b. Click on **Color Schemes**—every design has multiple color combinations for background, titles of slides and text. You can choose one that appeals to you **or** you can customize your color scheme. Click on **Edit Color Schemes** at bottom of Task Pane to give you even more design options.

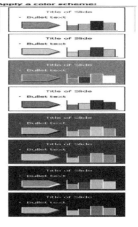

i. Edit Color Schemes.

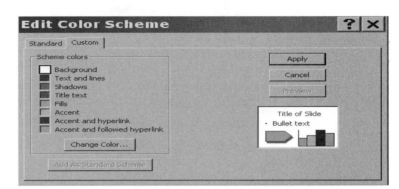

ii. The most important colors to set here are the **Background, Text and lines,** and **Title Text**.

iii. Highlight the color item you wish to change and click on the **Change Color** button.

Make sure you select high contrast colors. If you use a dark background, then select a light text color; if you use a light background, use a dark text color.

c. When you are finished exploring all the color options, click cancel in the dialog boxes to go back to the original blue, green, white combo choice as the color scheme for the Capsule design that will be applied for all slides in the show. When you choose a new slide layout, it will open with this design shown.

8. **Master Slide—View>>Master>>Slide Master** gives you the opportunity to add items such as objects, images, page numbers, and running titles to every slide in your show at once. This is where you create the consistent appearance that ties all of your slides together.

With a consistent appearance for each slide, the audience is able to more easily know where the next piece of information will be appearing. They will then focus on you and not on figuring out your slides.

The slide master looks like this:

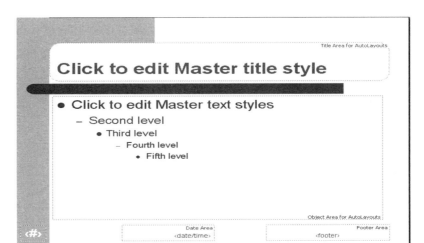

Let's make a master slide for our annual agency report:

a. For footer area, go to **View>>Header/Footer**

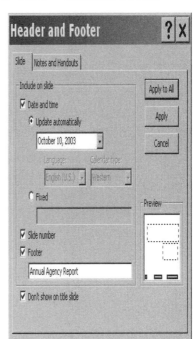

    i. Select date and time and update auto

    ii. Select slide number

    iii. Select footer and type *Annual Agency Report*

    iv. Check **Don't show on title slide**

    v. Click Apply to all

b. Add the tree logo from the agency letterhead:

    i. Open agency letterhead in new office document window, copy trees, and close.

    ii. Paste trees into upper right corner of slide master and reduce size to about 1".

c. Double click on page number in lower left and resize to 14 pt. on format menu.

d. Close Master View toolbar.

9. Click on **slide 2** in Outline Pane and note how the master slide background is now on this slide. It will be on every new slide you create.

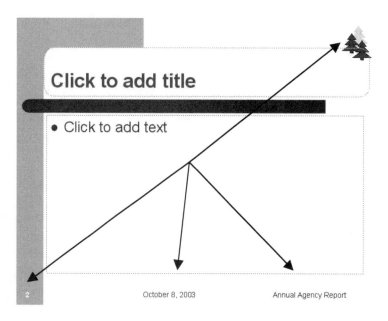

10. Because you checked **Don't show on title slide**, none of the footer data appears on the title slide. Click on slide 1 to check this out.

11. **Save** your work as *Alpine Annual Report 1* to ITSW folder, but do not close.

BUILDING YOUR PRESENTATION

Slide 1: Title

In this slide you will practice how to:
- Use WordArt to make a custom title.
- Utilize the colors from your color scheme design for subheadings and apply font formatting.
- Insert a text box from the Draw toolbar.

1. Select Slide 1 from outline pane.

2. WordArt Title: Insert WordArt from Draw Tool

   a. If Draw toolbar is not present, go to **View>>Toolbars and select Draw**

   b. Select **Row4:Column3** design

   c. Change font size to 60 pt., highlight existing text and type *Annual Agency Report*. Click OK.

   d. Select and cut the existing **Click to add title area**.

   e. Move your WordArt title to that space.

   f. When you click on this title, the WordArt toolbar appears.

      1) Click on the format icon

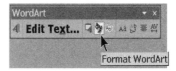

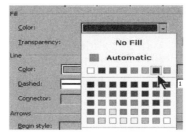

2) **Fill>>color** choose the dark blue from color scheme in drop down menu. Click OK.

3. Go to **Click to add subtitle**, go to **Format>>Font** and choose the following: Arial Black, 24 pt. bold italic, and select dark green. Click OK. Type *Alpine Community Mental Health* Center in this box. Select this text and center it.

4. Add **text box** from Draw toolbar below bar graphic. Type *2004* formatted as in #3.

5. The result:

6. In the outline/slide pane, click on **Outline**. Note that the report title does not appear; it is an image created in WordArt. The same is true for the date created by the text box. The only text on this slide is the agency name.

Slide 2: Agenda

In this slide you will learn how to:
- Use the Outlining toolbar
- Insert text on slides in the Outline view
- Employ line spacing to evenly align the text on the slide

1. Click on Side 2 in outline pane.

2. Go to **View>>Toolbars>>Outlining** to activate this toolbar.

3. In the Outline pane next to the slide, type *Agenda*

4. Hit enter and select demote in outline toolbar and type:

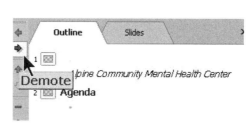

Agency Description
Employees' Salary Review
Client Profiles
Topic Highlight: Enhancing Social Services with IT

Whatever text you type in the outline pane is automatically placed on the slide pane and vice versa.

5. You notice that the agenda items are not vertically aligned on the slide. You can fix this using **line spacing.**

a. Select the text in box in slide pane and go to **Format>>Line Spacing>>2**. Click OK.

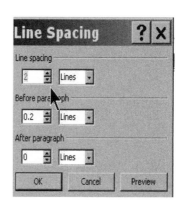

b. You may need to experiment to get the right spacing you want on slides you create. Use the preview button before you click OK.

6. The result:

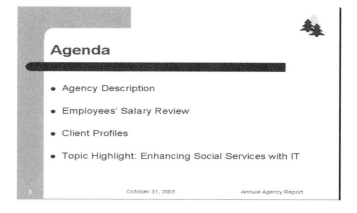

Slide 3: Agency Description

In this slide you will learn how to:
- Match slide layout to your data.
- Practice your formatting skills.

1. You want to list the services of the agency under two main headings. For this purpose, two columns would be appropriate. View>> task pane, select **Slide Layout>>Title and 2-Column text.**

2. In title bar type: *Agency Description*

3. In 1st column, type: (delete bullet first) *To provide prevention, early intervention and treatment services to the people of Northern Arizona in the areas of:*
   - *Substance abuse*
   - *Mental health*
   - *Child and family issues*

4. In the 2nd column, type: (delete bullet first) *Specific services include:*
   - *Information and referral*
   - *Outpatient counseling*
   - *Educational community programs*
   - *24 hr. hotline*

5. The result: What did I do? Play at formatting….

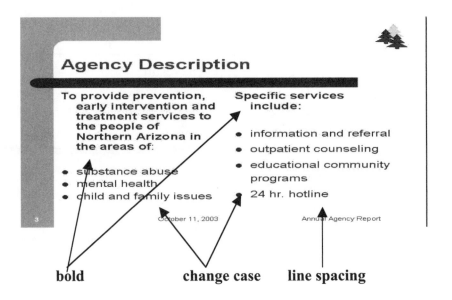

Slide 4: Employee Salary Review

In this slide you will learn how to:
- Use the notes pane.
- Insert a chart from another file.
- Manipulate paste options.
- Move and resize chart.

1. Select **New slide>>Title Only.** You need a blank area to paste your salary projections chart that you have already created.

2. Type in title area: *Employee Salary Review*

3. You will be asking the Board for a salary increase for the staff. It would be an aid to you if you had the text prepared.

   Type the following in the **Notes Pane** (below Slide Pane)**:**

   You are being asked to review and decide on proposed salary increases for our employees. A market analysis of salaries at comparable agencies within our state reveals that our staff is grossly underpaid. They are asking for a 3% increase. This increase would cost the agency...

4. Copy and paste the Salary Projection chart from your **Alpine Salary Projections** file in your ITSW folder.

   a. Minimize your presentation file.

   b. Find and open your Alpine Salary Projections file.

   c. Select and copy the salary chart and close this file.

   d. Maximize your presentation file. Click in open space on slide and click paste. A paste options icon appears in lower right of slide. Click on carrot and select **Picture of Table.**

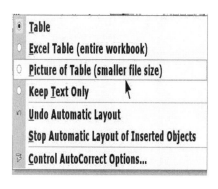

   e. Move and resize chart to fit slide space in text area.

5. The result:

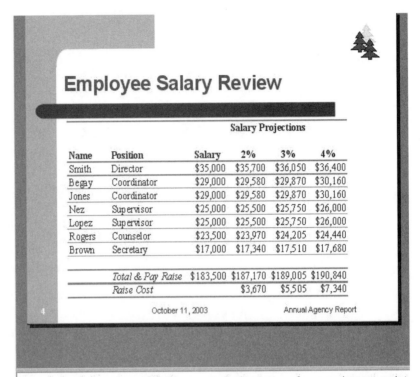

You are being asked to review and decide on proposed salary increases for our employees. A market analysis of salaries at comparable agencies within our state reveal that our staff is grossly underpaid. They are asking for a 3% increases. This increase would cost the agency.....

Slides 5-7: Client Profiles

The next three slides will introduce you to **chart creation** directly on a slide in PowerPoint. These slides profile client demographic distribution for the Board. They include data on ethnicity, geographic location, and problem code. Visuals of these data help in the determination of future program planning.

In these slides, you will learn how to:
- Create charts in PP.
- Enter data directly into the spreadsheet table.
- Practice formatting chart elements.

Slide 5: Ethnicity

1. Select **New Slide>>Title, Chart and Text.**

2. In title area type: *Client Profile*

3. You will create a chart showing the ethnic distribution of the clients in the agency

    a. Double click on chart and the default datasheet appears.

    b. Click in top left corner of chart to select all. Go to **Edit>>Clear>>all.**

    c. Type the following:

    remember to click on line to expand the column

		A
		Clients
1	Anglo	75
2	Hispanic	50
3	Native American	35
4	African American	10
5	Other	17

Alpine Annual Repc

    d. Close data sheet

    e. Format chart by double clicking in chart area. Chart options appear. Remember these skills? Modify as follows: move legend to bottom, change its font size to 14 pt., shadow its border, show value from data label tab <u>on</u> each column, change color on NA bar, and expand chart size to right (you can overlap the text box).

4. Type *Ethnic Distribution* in text area: remove bullet, align right, and vertical align at middle by grabbing textbox and moving it.

5. The result:

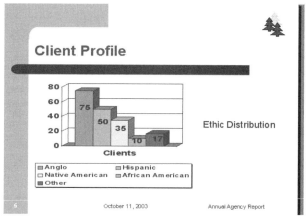

Slide 6: Geographic Distribution

1. Select **New Slide>>Title, Chart and Text.**

2. In title area type: *Client Profile*

3. You will create a chart showing the geographic distribution of the clients in the agency

   a. Double click on chart and the default datasheet appears.

   b. Click in top left corner of chart to select all. Go to **Edit>>Clear>>all.**

   c. Type the following:

		A
		Clients
1	Sedona	23
2	Williams	30
3	W. Flagstaff	67
4	W. Flagstaff	98
5	Sunnyside	63
6	Continental	43

   d. Close data sheet.

   e. Format chart by double clicking in chart area. Chart options appear. Modify as follows: move legend to bottom; change its font size to 14 pt., shadow its border, show value from data label tab above each column, change shape of bars to **4**, and expand chart size to right (you can overlap the text box).

4. Type *Geographic Distribution* in text area: remove bullet, align right, and vertical align at middle.

5. The result:

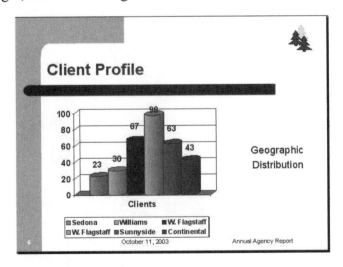

Slide 7: Problem Code

1. Select **New Slide>>Title, Chart and Text.**

2. In title area type: *Client Profile*

3. You will create a chart showing the problem code of the clients in the agency

   a. Double click on chart and the default datasheet appears.

   b. Click in top left corner of chart to select all. Go to **Edit>>Clear>>all.**

   c. Type the following:

			A
			Clients
1		Substance Abuse	250
2		Mental Health	199
3		Family Issues	75

   d. Close data sheet.

   e. Format chart by double clicking in chart area. Chart options appear. Replicate the formatting from the image of the chart in #5.

4. Type *Problem Code* in text area: remove bullet, align right, and vertical align at middle.

5. The result:

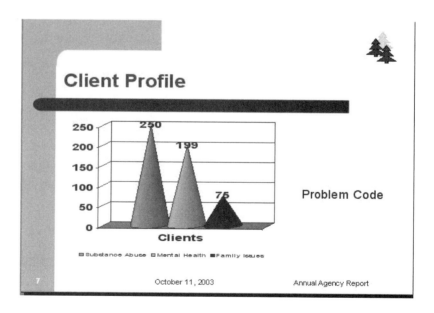

Slide 8: Topic Highlight

In this last slide you will learn how to:
- Insert AutoShapes.
- Practice the fill and line tools on the Draw toolbar.

1. You are going to discuss with the Board how the use of IT enhances agency functioning and client services. You will need two columns.

2. Click on **New Slide>>Title and 2-Column Text.**

3. Type *Enhancing Social Services with IT* in 1st column and remove bullet.

4. Change bullet type and type in 2nd column. Enlarge text box so that each item fits on one line:
   - *Agency Templates*
   - *Computerized I&R Directory*
   - *Visual Client Evaluation*
   - *"What If" Scenarios*
   - *Evidence Based Practice*

5. Format all text in Arial, 24 pt., bold and dark blue.

6. Increase line spacing for 2nd column to 1.75.

7. In 1st column, go to Draw toolbar and click on **AutoShapes>>Block Arrows>>Striped Right Arrow** and make it about 1" long and .5" wide, in middle of text box, color it dark purple with a dark blue line around the fill.

8. Move *Enhancing Social Services* above this arrow and *with IT* below it.

9. The result:

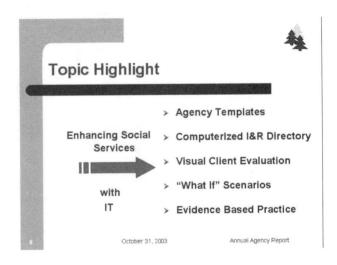

ADDING ANIMATION TO THE SLIDE SHOW

Let's see how your slide presentation to the Board looks on the big screen. View the show by clicking on slide 1 on the outline pane and then clicking on the slide show icon on the shortcut bar. Left click on your mouse to move to the next slide.

While it looks good, it lacks pizzazz. You need to animate the slides to really engage the audience. You do this by adding **transition effects** between slides and on individual slides.

There are two types of transitions:

1. **Slide Transition:** determines how each slide looks when it first appears.
2. **Custom Animation:** how your text, pictures, charts, etc. appear on each slide.

Slide transitions

1. Go to **Slide Transition** menu option in task pane.

2. It is best that all slides have the same visual transition; otherwise the visual will dominant your presentation and people will not listen to you. Select **Box Out.**

3. Choose a **slow** speed and **No** sound.

4. Advance slide **on mouse click** so you have control when to show the next slide.

5. Click **Apply to All Slides.** Click on **Slide Sorter** icon on Shortcut bar. Notice there is now a transition icon below each slide. Click on these icons to preview the effect.

Custom animation

You can make a slide first appear without any data or with only part of it revealed. By having this control, you engage the audience in what you are saying. They are not trying to read the entire slide while listening to you. Clicking on the mouse causes another chunk of data to appear. This procedure is called **custom animation.** You select it from the drop-down menu on the task pane.

We will uniquely animate each of our 8 slides. Each animation follows the same procedure: **select an element of the slide, and then click "Add Effect" to add animation.**

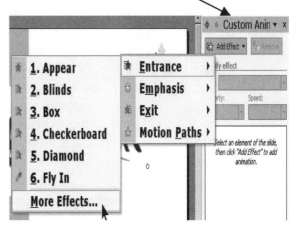

 Please don't get carried away with your new found skills in animation. Click on **More Effects...** to see what I mean.

 Decide in what order you want the slide elements to appear on the screen because it is easiest to animate them in order from the start.

Here we go:

1. Select Title Slide:
   a. Select the WordArt title:
      i. **Add Effect>>Entrance>>Diamond**
      ii. **Modify Diamond:**

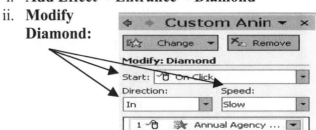

   b. Select agency name: **Entrance effect>>fly in>>from right>>fast**

c. Select year: **Entrance effect>>fly in>>from bottom>>fast**

Let's examine what you did:

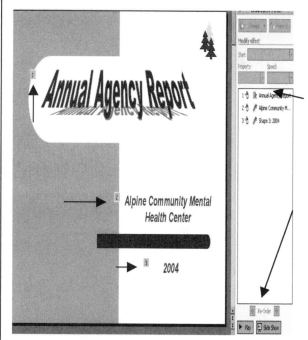

1) The three animation elements are numbered and ordered.

2) Clicking on any one of your animations will display all of its actions.

3) You can reorder the elements; or change or remove them.

4) You can preview any or all of your animations.

Once you understand how to do this, we can quickly move through the rest of the slides.

2. Slide 2: For both the *Agenda **and** Items,* select **Add Effect>>Entrance>>Fly In>>On Click>>From Left>>Fast.**

3. Slide 3:
    a. *Agency Description*: **Add Effect>>Entrance>>Fly In>>On Click>>From Left>> Fast.**
    b. *1st Column:* **Add Effect>>Entrance>>Fly In>> On Click>>From Left>>Fast.**
    c. *2nd Column:* **Add Effect>>Entrance>>Fly In>> On Click>>From Right>>Fast.**

4. Slide 4:
    a. *Employee Salary Review:* **Add Effect>>Entrance>>Fly In>>On Click>>From Left>>Fast.**
    b. Chart (object)*:* **Add Effect>>Entrance>>Box>> On Click>>Out>>Fast.**

5. Slides 5-7: You will make each bar in graph appear one at a time. This will enable you to discuss each demographic individually before moving onto the next statistic. You want the slide title and the type of demographic to appear before the graph so you will click on the chart to animate last in the order.

Follow these steps for all three slides:

a. Slide Title: **Add Effect>>Entrance>>Fly In>>On Click>>From Left>>Fast**
b. Slide Demographic: **Add Effect>>Entrance>>Fly In>>On Click>>From Right>>Fast**
c. Chart: **Add Effect>>Entrance>>Appear**
d. Click on carrot next to chart box in task pane and choose **Effect Options**

e. Select **Chart Animation>>By element in series** and click OK.
f. Click on slide show starting with slide 5 to see how the elements of the graph appear with each mouse click.

 To exit the slide show, hit the ESC key in the upper left of your keyboard

6. Slide 8:
    a. *Topic Highlight*: **Add Effect>>Entrance>>Fly In>>On Click>>From Left>>Fast**
    b. *Enhancing Social Services with IT*: **Add Effect>>Entrance>>Appear**
    c. *Arrow:* **Add Effect>>Entrance>>Blinds>>On Click>>Horizontal>>Fast**
    d. *2nd Column Text:*
        i. **Add Effect>>Entrance>>Fly In>>On Click>>From Right>>Fast**

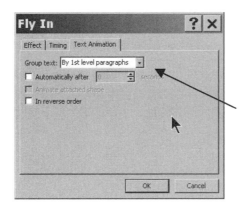

ii. Click on carrot next to text box in task pane and choose **Effect Options**

iii. Select **Text Animation>>By 1st level paragraphs** and click OK

7. Save your file in ITSW folder.

RUN THE SLIDE SHOW NOW!

DISPLAYING THE SHOW

1. You can rehearse the delivery of your presentation. PP times it for you. **Slide Show>>Rehearse Timings.**

2. There are many shortcut keys that can help you during the slide show. You can access a full list of them by pressing the F1 key while in the Slide Show mode.

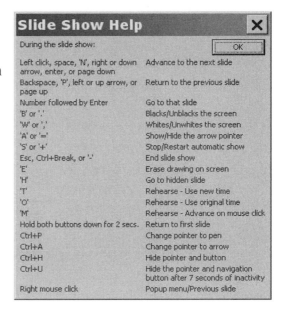

3. There are two very useful shortcuts:

   a. Pressing the **B key** during a presentation turns the screen black; pressing it again brings it back to where is was. This can very useful when you want the audience focus on you and not the slides.

   b. Pressing the **A key** makes the pointer appear; pressing it again makes it disappear. This is very useful when you want to emphasize a point on your slides.

4. Slide Navigation. By right clicking your mouse during the slide show, you can navigate around your presentation. This is particularly useful if you want to move to another slide or perform other options.

PRINTING THE SHOW

You have several options for printing your presentation.

1. Slides: prints slides as seen on screen.
2. Handouts: choose maximum of 3 slides/page for best viewing; lines for notes are printed next to each slide.
3. Notes Pages: this option is for your personal use.
4. Outline: provides only the text for each slide.

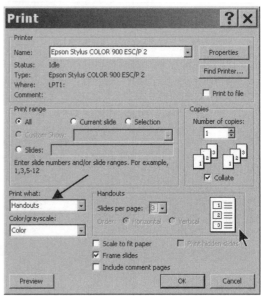

Endnote

You have spent approximately the last fifteen weeks learning the skills of information technology. You have learned the uses of various IT tools in effective work with clients and in agency tasks. Practice, practice, practice! As with any skill, you will become rusty and "loose it" if you do not use it. Choi, Ligon, and Ward (2002) state "with the continued refinement of software and hardware and the burgeoning Internet, it is imperative that social workers capitalize on the potential for technology to maximize the effectiveness of our agencies and their services" (p. 10).

Hopefully, this immersion has given you the confidence and competence to now think of yourself as a 21st century social worker.

Glossary

This glossary is not meant to be inclusive of all the terms and concepts you encounter in this book. Instead, view it as a beginning point for you in which you might add your own definitions. In addition, many of the terms pertaining to the Internet and its related areas are already defined in the glossary in the *Research Navigator Guide for the Helping Professions* (pages 247-250) and need not be duplicated here.

A

Absolute Cell Value Also called absolute cell reference within the Excel program. When you want to use some of the information that the original formula uses when you copy the formula, you indicate this with a $ sign before the column letter and row number. It visually looks like this: =$A$1*C4 where the actual value in A1 is used in all subsequent calculations.

AutoCorrect Automatically detects and corrects typos, misspelled words, and incorrect capitalization. To activate and customize this function go to the Tools menu of every program in MS Office.

B

Browser A software program, such as Internet Explorer, that can display WWW documents. They "translate" HTML-encoded files into the text, images, sounds, and other features you see. Another browser you might be using is Netscape.

BTEAM An acronym for the five roles of a social worker, including broker, teacher, enabler, advocate, and mediator.

C

Catchment Area A geographic area identified by a social service agency in which it provides its services.

CD-ROM A type of disc that stores up to one gigabyte of data. The disc can also be used to backup data on hard drives because of their large storage capacity.

D

Database A large pool of organized information available to the user. The information can be manipulated by sorting, filters, and/or queries. This allows the user to select only the information the user seeks. A database program such as Access is very powerful in that you can create forms for easy data entry, and queries and reports from the data.

Defragment See **fragmentation**.

Document template See **template.**

Domain Describes the site type of the URL you are visiting; these types include .gov, .edu, .org., and .com. The type alerts you to the degree of information validity or trust you can have about the site's contents.

E

Ecomap A visual aid used by social workers with their clients that depict the person-in-environment contexts of the client, including all environmental (systemic) influences. The reciprocal nature of these influences is shown by various intensity and direction of lines and arrows.

E-mail Short for electronic mail. These messages can be sent anywhere in the world over the Internet.

F

Floppy Disk A removable storage disk that can hold up to 1.44mb of data. It is commonly used to transfer information between computers and to backup small amounts of data.

Fragmentation When data is deleted from a hard drive, the data is not actually removed. It leaves a blank space on the drive. When you create new files or copy and paste files, they are placed at the end of the drive or in these empty spaces. Not all the empty spaces are filled in, however. This leads to the drive moving through these spaces to find actual files. The empty spaces fragment the disk and slow down the processing of files. Defragmentation rewrites the data on the drive so it is contiguous, eliminating the empty spaces.

G

Genogram A diagram depicting family relationships extended over generations. Circles for women and squares for men are used together with vertical lines to indicate marriages, divorces, births, and deaths. A genogram's major purpose is to show recurrent patterns of behavior.

H

Hard Drive Disk, generally located inside your CPU, where data and programs are stored.

Hardware The physical machinery—the computer, keyboard, monitor, printer, and other devices—designed for entering, storing, processing, and transmitting data.

I

Information Technology The use of computer and web applications and tools.

Internet An immense series of globally networked computers in which any computer can communicate with another computer as long as they are connected to the network.

There are several ways that they communicate, including using e-mail and the Web. The term is not synonymous with the Web. See **Web**.

M

Mail Merge A process in a word processing program that allows you to create and then print form letters, labels, or envelopes from an organized list usually taken from a spreadsheet or database program.

MS Office Microsoft Office is a suite of programs that include: Word, Excel, PowerPoint, and Outlook for the Standard Edition. Publisher and Small Business Edition Tools are included in the Small Business Edition, and FrontPage and Access are added to the Professional Edition. The Professional Edition is recommended for agency use.

Multi-tasking Working on more than one computer task at the same time. For example, having more than one application open at once and then copying and pasting images between documents.

O

On-line A system for communicating with a central computer processor (or server), usually to retrieve, send, or store information. On-line systems permit personal computer users with connections to the internet through hardware devices such as modems, cable modems, or Ethernet connections.

Q

Queries Locates specific information according to special criteria in databases. They answer specific questions and are more powerful than filters in that they can isolate a group of records plus limit the fields to be included. Queries can be saved in the database file you are working in.

R

RAM (random access memory) Memory where programs are run and data is stored while the date is being manipulated.

S

Significance There are three kinds of significance in client evaluation: visual—the actual observing of change in the charting of client target behaviors; practical—the change in target behavior of a client system from a clinical or substantive viewpoint; and statistical—the probability that the change in target behavior occurred because of intervention and not errors of measurement or chance.

Single Case Design Also called single subject design. Both a research and a practice tool used to evaluate client progress. Target behaviors are identified mutually between client and worker. They are measured during a baseline period which can be days or weeks and then intervention is introduced to affect change in these behaviors. Measurement continues during this phase and the degree of change as noted by frequency, intensity, or magnitude is observed. Intervention is stopped by mutual agreement of worker and client when the changes are deemed satisfactory. A period of measurement, the second baseline, in which no intervention is occurring, is taken. This second baseline is to ensure that the changes made have taken. Then and only then should termination occur. The beauty of this form of evaluation is that a different intervention can be introduced if it is ineffective. This design is created in a spreadsheet.

Social Network Map Used to assess a client's social support network, a social network map illustrates the structure and function of a client's social networks. Its major purpose is to point out the relevant strengths of and barriers to social support networks for clients.

Software The programs (or instructions) that make the physical equipment (or hardware) execute the desired operations.

Spreadsheet An electronic ledger that allows you to enter and manipulate numbers. Most common use is for budgeting, but it also provides the ability to do forecasting, also known as "what if" scenarios, in which you can predict the outcome of certain situations before they happen. This is particularly useful for salary projections or client number increases to plan for new programs and/or location of services. Spreadsheets also provide the framework for client evaluation.

T

Taskbar The bar along the bottom of your screen in which appears the Start button, the Quick Launch bar (if activated), the buttons for all active programs, the current system time, and the system tray.

Task Pane Access important operations from a single location, usually on the right side of your screen. Perform searches, open files, view the Office Clipboard, format documents and presentations, download templates, and complete other tasks.

Template A preformatted blank document that contains text, images, and/or styles that you created and saved. Usually used for forms, letterheads, memos, resumes, and other documents that you repeatedly use. It eliminates the need to go a printing supply store to purchase them, plus you can customize them to your own needs.

Telehealth An electronic network of video machines wherein mental health professionals and clients can see and hear one another for the purposes of assessment and intervention. This mode of providing outpatient services is especially useful in rural areas where the participants would have to travel many miles to see one another. Besides client services, this technology is also used for professional development of staff and interoffice or interagency meetings.

U

URL Uniform Resource Locator. The unique global address of documents on the Web. There is a logic to the layout of a URL: For example, the URL for Northern Arizona University is http://www.nau.edu where http is the protocol; www is World Wide Web; nau is location of the site; and edu is the site type.

Utility Programs   In the use of computers, the programs that help in the general running of the system for such things as transferring data from one storage site to another; making copies of files; locating and eliminating viruses; and saving data.

W

Web   Also known as World Wide Web (www). It is a way of accessing information over the medium of the Internet using the http protocol. This protocol always looks like this: http://www.(the web address) which indicates a specific location or website on the Web. The Internet is not synonymous with the Web. See **Internet**.

"What if" scenarios   A spreadsheet task that will predict the outcome of some problem, issue or project using formulas. It is used as an aid to decision-making.

Wizard   A program that guides you through the steps involved in executing a complex task such as mail merge or chart creation in Microsoft Office.

References

Bisman, C. & Hardcastle, D. (1999). Integrating Research Into Practice- A Model of Effective Social Work. Belmont, CA: Wadsworth.

Bogal-Allbritten, R. & Allbritten, W. (1985). A Computer Literacy Course for Students and Professionals in Human Services. Journal of College Student Personnel, 26(2), 170-171.

Brown, C. (2001), Microsoft Officexp Plain and Simple. Redmond. WA: Microsoft Press.

Butterfield, W. (1983). Computers for Social Work Practitioners. Practice Digest, 6(3), Entire Issue.

Cnaan, R. (1989). Social work education and direct practice in the computer age. Journal of Social Work Education, 25(3), 235-43.

Cournoyer, B. (2004). The Evidence-Based Social Work Skills Book. Boston: Allyn & Bacon.

Choi, G., Ligon, J. & Ward, J. (2002). Computer Anxiety and Social Workers: Differences by Access, Use and Training. Journal of Technology in Human Services, 19(1), 1-12.

Friedman, B., Ward, D. & Biagianti, A. (1998). Enhancing student ability to navigate the rapidly changing information environment. Paper presented at the 42nd Annual Program Meeting of the Council on Social Work Education, Chicago, Il.

Finn, J. & Lavitt, M. (1995). A Survey of Information Technology-Related Curriculum in Undergraduate Social Work Programs. The Journal of Baccalaureate Social Work, 1(1), 39-53.

Finn, J. (1988). Microcomputers in Private Nonprofit Agencies: A Survey of Utilization Trends and Training Requirements. Computer Use in Social Services Network Newsletter, 8/9(4/1), 27-32.

Gibbs, L. (2003). Evidence-Based Practice for the Helping Professions. Pacific Grove, CA: Brooks/Cole.

Gibson, S., Morley, S. & Romeo-Wolff, C. (2002). A Model Community Telepsychiatry Program in Rural Arizona. In R. Hsiung, E-Therapy: Case Studies, Guiding Principles, and the Clinical Potential of the Internet (pp. 69-91). New York: W.W. Norton & Company.

Gingerich, W. & Green, T. (1996). Information Technology: How Social Work is Going Digital. In P. Raffoul, Future Issues for Social Work Practice (pp. 19-28). Boston: Allyn & Bacon.

Glastonbury, B., LaMendola, W. & Toole, S. (1988). Information technology and the human services. Chichester, Great Britain: John Wiley & Sons.

Grant, G. & Grobman, L. (1998). The Social Worker's Internet Handbook. Harrisburgh, PA: White Hat Communications.

Hartman, A. (1978). Diagrammatic assessment of family relationships. Social Casework, 59, 456-476.

Hartman, A. & Laird, J. (1983). Family Centered Social Work Practice. New York: The Free Press.

Kardas, E. & Milford, T. (1996). Using the Internet for Social Science Research and Practice. Belmont, CA: Wadsworth.

Karger, H. & Levine, J. (1999). The Internet and technology for the human services. Reading, MS: Addison Wesley Longman, Inc.

Kinkoph, S. et. Al. (2003). Making the Most of Your Windows PC. Indianapolis, Indiana: Que Publishing.

Kjosness, J. & Barr, L. (2004). Research Navigator Guide for the Helping Professions. Boston: Allyn & Bacon.

Mattaini, M. (1993). More Than a Thousand Words: Graphics for Clinical Practice. Washington, D.C.: NASW Press.

Marks, R. (2002). Harnessing the Evidence from the Tulane School of Social Work's 2002 Deans Report. Retrieved October 17, 2003 from the World Wide Web: http://www.tulane.edu/~tssw/new/School/DeansReport02.pdf.

Marlow, C. (2001). Research Methods for Generalist Social Work. Belmont, CA: Wadsworth.

Martinez, R. & Clark, C. (2001). The Social Worker's Guide to the Internet. Needham Heights, MA: Allyn & Bacon.

Monnickendam, M. & Eaglstein, A. (1993). Computer acceptance by social workers: Some unexpected research findings. Computers in Human Services, 9, 409–424.

Miller, H. (1986). The Use of Computers in Social Practice: An Assessment. Journal of Social Work Education, 22(3), 52-60.

Miller-Cribbs, J. (Ed.). (2001). New Advances in Technology for Social Work Education and Practice. New York: Haworth.

NASW News. (1999). Five Added, 17 Revised. October, 1999. p. 8.

National Association of Social Workers. (2003). Social work speaks: National Association of Social Workers policy statements, 2003-2006—sixth ed. Washington, DC: NASW Press.

Neuman, W. & Kreuger, L. (2003). Social Work Research Methods: Qualitative and Quantitative Applications. Needham Heights, MA: Allyn & Bacon.

Nurius, P. Hooyman, N., & Nicoll, A. (1991). Computers in agencies: A survey baseline and planning implications. Journal of Social Service Research, 14, 141–155.

Pardek, J. , Dotson, G. , Ricketts, A. , McCully, K., & Lewis, A. (1995). Replication of a Study Exploring the Utilization of Computer Technology by Social Workers. The Clinical Supervisor, 13(2), 127-140.

Patterson, D. (2000). Personal Computer Applications in the Social Services. Boston: Allyn and Bacon.

Resnick, H. (ed.). (1994). Electronic Tools for Social Work Practice and Education. New York: Haworth.

Resnick, H. & Anderson, P. (eds.). (2002). Human Services Technology: Innovations in Practice and Education. New York: Haworth.

Rondero, V. (1998). Computer Technology in Social Work Settings: Issues, Considerations and Implications for the Profession. In Information Technology for Social Work Practitioner's and Educator's Conference Proceedings (pp. 40-50). Columbia, SC: School of Social Work, University of South Carolina.

Royse, D. (2004). Research Methods in Social Work. Belmont, CA: Wadsworth.

Rubin, A. & Babbie, E. (2001). Research Methods for Social Work (4th Ed.). Belmont, CA: Wadsworth.

Sheldon, B. (2001). The Validity of Evidence-Based Practice in Social Work. British Journal of Social Work, 31, 801-809.

Sheldon, B. & Chilvers, R. (2000). Evidence-Based Social Care: A study of prospects and problems. Lyme Regis: Russell House Publishing.

Schervish, P. (1993). Information Use by Levels in Human Service Organisations. Computers in Human Services, 9(3/4), 397-408.

Schoech, D. (1999). <u>Human Services Technology: Understanding, Designing, and Implementing Computer and Internet Applications in the Social Services.</u> New York: Haworth.

Taylor, C. (2002). What Works about What Works? Fashion, fad and EBP. <u>Social Work & Social Science Review</u>, 10(2), 63-81.

Tierney, S. (2002). Reframing an Evidence-Based Approach to Practice. <u>Social Work & Social Science Review</u>, 10(2), 49-62.

Tracy, E. (1993) Teaching about Social Networks and Social Support: A Social Network Mapping Exercise, <u>Journal of Teaching in Social Work</u>, 7(2), 37-36.

Tracy, E. & Whittaker, J. (1990). The social network map: Assessing social support in clinical practice. <u>Families in Society</u>, 71(8), 461-470.

Vernon, R. & Lynch, D. (2000). <u>Social Work and the Web</u>. Pacific Groves, CA: Wadsworth.

Wang, W. (2001). <u>Office for Dummies</u>. New York, NY: Wiley Publishing.

Yegidis, B. & Weinbach, R<u>. Research Methods for Social Workers (4th Ed.).</u> Needham Heights, MA: Allyn & Bacon.

Index

Index

Index

NOTES

NOTES

NOTES

NOTES

NOTES

NOTES